# ⌂ HOMEWORK 1: INSIDE

# ⌂ HOMEWORK 1: INSIDE

Structures Publishing Company
Farmington, Michigan 48024

**Editor** Shirley  Horowitz

**Graphics Editor** Carey Jean Ferchland

Current Printing (last digit)
10   9   8   7   6   5   4   3   2   1


Original Copyright © German Edition

Orbis Verlag/Verlagsgruppe Bertelsmann
2 Hamburg
Konrad Adenauerallee 9
WEST GERMANY

# List of Projects

Quick & Easy Coffee Table . . . . . . . . . . . . . . . . . . . . . . . . . . . . . . . . . . 8
The *Selbermachen* Dowel System . . . . . . . . . . . . . . . . . . . . . . . . . . . 11
Easier Furniture Building . . . . . . . . . . . . . . . . . . . . . . . . . . . . . . . . . . 17
Flower-Power in the Living Room . . . . . . . . . . . . . . . . . . . . . . . . . . 23
Curio Display Case . . . . . . . . . . . . . . . . . . . . . . . . . . . . . . . . . . . . . . . 26
A First Car Just Like Dad's . . . . . . . . . . . . . . . . . . . . . . . . . . . . . . . . 30
Bunk-Bed Tower Maximizes Living Space . . . . . . . . . . . . . . . . . . 33
Living Room Storage Wall Can Move With You . . . . . . . . . . . . . . 38
The Tri-Level Table . . . . . . . . . . . . . . . . . . . . . . . . . . . . . . . . . . . . . . 42
Child's Movie Theater . . . . . . . . . . . . . . . . . . . . . . . . . . . . . . . . . . . 44
Conversation Pit . . . . . . . . . . . . . . . . . . . . . . . . . . . . . . . . . . . . . . . . 47
Picking up with Mr. Cleanup . . . . . . . . . . . . . . . . . . . . . . . . . . . . . . 52
Sideboard with Rolling Serving Carts . . . . . . . . . . . . . . . . . . . . . . 54
The Little Engineer:
    Night-express Through the Playroom . . . . . . . . . . . . . . . . . . . . 60
A Practical Bed for Your Guests . . . . . . . . . . . . . . . . . . . . . . . . . . . 63
Settee and Chair of Wood and Sisal Cord . . . . . . . . . . . . . . . . . . 66
A Cabinet With a Twist . . . . . . . . . . . . . . . . . . . . . . . . . . . . . . . . . . 69
A Roomful of Furniture for $240 . . . . . . . . . . . . . . . . . . . . . . . . . . 72
A Children's Table with Muscles . . . . . . . . . . . . . . . . . . . . . . . . . . 77
Clever Max for Children . . . . . . . . . . . . . . . . . . . . . . . . . . . . . . . . . 81
From Out of the Box: An Extra Bed! . . . . . . . . . . . . . . . . . . . . . . . 84
A Handy Party Table . . . . . . . . . . . . . . . . . . . . . . . . . . . . . . . . . . . . 88
A Bookshelf as Big as You Want It to Be . . . . . . . . . . . . . . . . . . . . 91
Living Room Furniture; Build It Fast but Solid . . . . . . . . . . . . . . . 92
The Shelves That Turn the Corner . . . . . . . . . . . . . . . . . . . . . . . . . 96
Swinging Flowers . . . . . . . . . . . . . . . . . . . . . . . . . . . . . . . . . . . . . . .101
Modular Table: Little or Really Big! . . . . . . . . . . . . . . . . . . . . . . . .102
Combination Cabinet and Table for Children . . . . . . . . . . . . . . .105
Versatile Wall Unit . . . . . . . . . . . . . . . . . . . . . . . . . . . . . . . . . . . . . .110

# Foreword

The **HOMEWORK** series is a refreshing new approach to do-it-yourself projects. I call it **HOMEWORK** because the work is done at home with home workshop tools, and because the projects are all connected with the home in some way.

The first two volumes, **HOMEWORK 1: INSIDE** and **HOMEWORK 2: OUTSIDE**, are a distillation of the series called "Selbermachen" created by a German publisher, subtitled, "The Practical Handbook for Practical People." The selections for these two books represent the most attractive projects for English-language homeworkers, chosen from the five much larger "Selbermachen" volumes.

Future **HOMEWORK** books will be from the Selbermachen series and other foreign sources, as well as extracts from U.S. magazines not previously published in book form. We think we have found, and will find, more exciting and ingenious projects that will give the homeworker hours of rewarding work as well as finished projects the family can enjoy for years to come.

Since discovering the "Selbermachen" books at the Frankfurt International Book Fair, I have been humbled by the task that I undertook. The first step was to carefully select projects which would interest English-language homeworkers. Next, the text and the dimensions had to be translated from German.

Then, it fell to me as the author of "The American Metric Construction Handbook" to translate the translation. This means the translation of European sizes had to be converted to usages available and accepted in the U.S. and Canada.

For example, the text may call for a wood member that translates from the metric as $1^{15}/_{16}$" x $2^{7}/_{8}$"; there is no comparable U.S. size. But we do have a 2" x 3" ($1\frac{1}{2}$ x $2\frac{1}{2}$), so that a judgment must be made as to whether the 2" x 3" will do the job and whether abutting materials can accommodate a size change.

Most of this work has fallen to me and I beg your indulgence if you find an occasional error. Before you begin to assemble a project, it would be well to check to see that everything fits together, particularly if you choose to alter any dimension. If you find an error, or a better way to do it, please let me know, so we may modify future printings.

Why don't we show metric dimensions as well as inches? There are two reasons: some metric material sizes have not been determined in the U.S., and metric materials may not be available at your local source for some years.

We hope that you have many hours of recreation building these projects, and that you and yours will enjoy their beauty and utility in years to come.

R. J. Lytle
*Publisher*

# Quick & easy coffee table

This table is made of glass, plexiglass and aluminum tubing and will go with any modern furnishings. Construction can be easily completed in one weekend. Saw, drill, slit, and tighten screws — that's all.

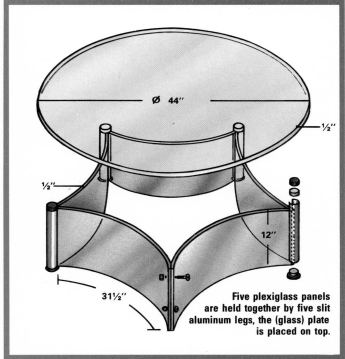

Five plexiglass panels are held together by five slit aluminum legs, the (glass) plate is placed on top.

The homemade gauge at left is a requirement for the accurate and even production of the five table legs. It must correspond to the diameter and length of the legs.

Sawing, slitting, tightening screws and assembling — that's all you have to do to construct this table. The assembly is done quickly and handily: You do not need to wait until glue has set or paint has dried. Form and color are determined solely by the material: Plexiglass, aluminum tubing and glass. It is best to order the table top from a glazer, entirely according to taste; choose clear glass or smoked glass, diameter 44 in. x ½ in. thick. The five plexiglass segments of the pedestal are screwed together and secured by means of pieces of slit-open aluminum tubing.

The aluminum tubing must be cut open neatly. With the homemade gauge, this is no problem at all. It is exactly as long as each leg (12'') and is built

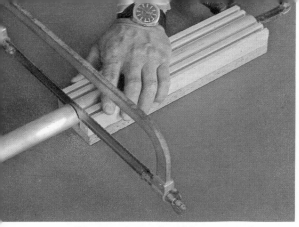

The gauge is exactly 12" long, as are the table legs. Thus you do not have to measure anew each time a leg is cut.

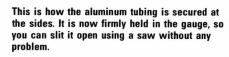
This is how the aluminum tubing is secured at the sides. It is now firmly held in the gauge, so you can slit it open using a saw without any problem.

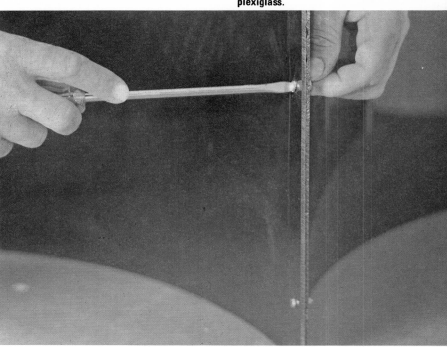
The saw blade of the circular saw used to cut the tubing has been changed to a cutting disk which must be double the thickness of the plexiglass.

This is how to avoid scratches in the plexiglass: bottom and side contact surfaces of the saw are covered with felt strips.

The plexiglass segments are connected with two screws each. The pentagon shape is created automatically through tension in the material.

The tubing is pushed over the screw-connected plexiglass segments. Since the screws are on the inside, it cannot slip off.

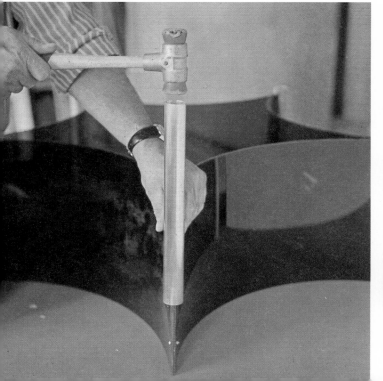

## MATERIALS
5 Plexiglass segments,
32 x 12 x ⅛" each.
5 legs, aluminum tubing,
12" x 1⅛" diameter
Wooden disks, felt padding,
screws and nuts.
Diameter of the table top:
44 x ½" thick

of a piece of pressed woo and two strips of wood Dimensions of the inne edges: ⅛ in. each. Th plexiglass segments ma be purchased precut, or yo can cut them yourself. A li tle oil, dribbled onto th cutting line, will result in clean edge. Also make template for drilling th screw holes, so that a screws are placed at a even height. Distance t outer edge: $^{19}/_{32}$". Th pieces of tubing are pushe onto the frame, which i connected by screws an closed off at the top an bottom with wooden plug Felt disks are placed on to as a resting basis for th plate glass.

The tubing is closed off on top and at the bottom with wooden plugs. A felt disk is placed on top as support for the table top.

The basic construction. Square posts are drilled uniformly. Dowels are the connecting elements between the various parts.

Here's what it looks like inside the posts. Notched dowels are secured with a 2⅜" long dowel pin.

# The *Selbermachen* Dowel System

Furniture building without glue, screws or nails! Yes, it can be done! With a dowel system developed by *SELBERMACHEN,* square parts are connected by dowels and secured by locking dowel pins, much like the corners of a log cabin. Many sturdy, functional pieces of furniture can be made. Illustrated here are three items that show the possibilities of this ingenious system.

Cabinet and chair,
two entirely different
pieces of furniture,
are made from the same
construction system.
With the aid of the
drill template
this and a number of
other furniture pieces
can easily be made by
the homeworker.

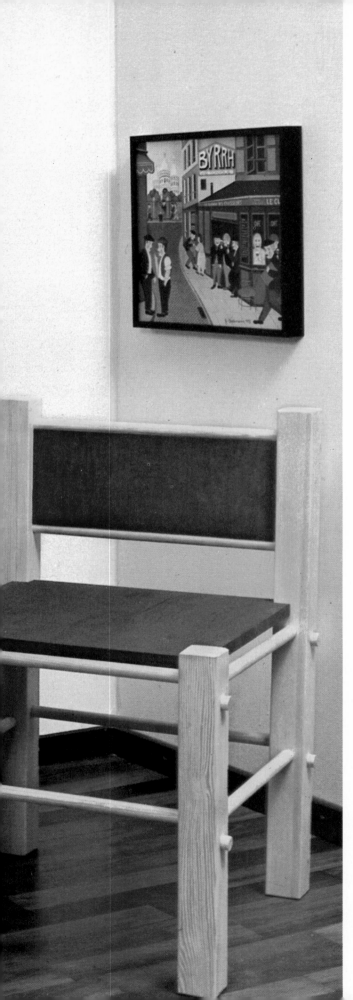

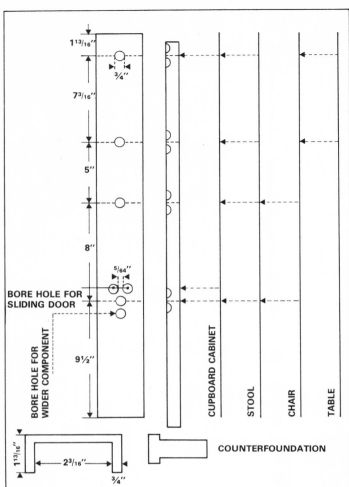

BORE HOLE FOR SLIDING DOOR

BORE HOLE FOR WIDER COMPONENT

$1^{13}/_{16}$"

$7^{3}/_{16}$"

5"

8"

$9^{1}/_{2}$"

$^{3}/_{4}$"

$^{5}/_{64}$"

CUPBOARD CABINET

STOOL

CHAIR

TABLE

$1^{13}/_{16}$"

$2^{3}/_{16}$"

$^{3}/_{4}$"

COUNTERFOUNDATION

**Making this drill-template is essential for our modular construction system. In three examples we show you a number of interesting applications for building various pieces of furniture.**

"First drill, then build" is the motto of the *SELBER-MACHEN* dowel system. The standard materials, square posts, dowels, and plywood or veneered particleboard, can be efficiently made into furniture with the aid of a template and drill press. These items of furniture are strong and can easily be disassembled, since they are neither screwed nor glued together.

Use ¾ in. plywood for the drill template. Cut two strips 31½ in. long. One is 2¼ in. wide and the other 3⅝ in. These two plywood strips are drilled with a ¾ in. drill or wood bit as shown in the drawing above. The 2³/₁₆ in. wide strip is sawn into two 1¹/₁₆ in. strips (about ⅛ in. is lost to the saw kerf) after drilling.

**The basic materials: square lumber 2³/₁₆" x 2³/₁₆", ¾" dowels, ¾" plywood. Also saw, drill, square and mallet.**

**Tool for pulling dowels out: two square pieces of lumber 2" x 2" nominal, 6" long, are connected with canvas webbing.**

## Correct handling of drill template

The template (see text for instructions on how to make template) is also used as the length standard. At 37½", it is a frequently used length in the Selbermachen system.

Place template flush onto the square wood and drill 1³¹/₃₂" deep with a ¾" bit in the drill press. Insert locking dowel pin into this hole (see below) and drill remaining holes with the aid of the template. This gives us the precise fit when the elements are assembled. Note: Dowel pins with a head as shown are not required.

A dowel is inserted into the first hole drilled. The square piece is then turned once and the template moved up by ⁹/₁₆". It now rests with the half-round cut-out on the dowel. By staggering the holes the individual dowels are locked into each other.

These are glued to the top of the wide template so that the half-round cut-outs, resulting from splitting the ¾ in. holes, point outward. The space between the template sides corresponds to the thickness of the square material. **Caution:** *here is one of the difficulties of translating Metric to English dimensions. In the U.S. you may have to resize the template to the stock or vice-versa.*

The square lumber, since it is not a standard U.S. size, will have to be made for you by a local millwork house. Or you may buy truck stakes or 4 x 4 (3½ in. x 3½ in.) lumber to cut it yourself if you have the equipment. Cut lumber to the proper lengths.

Place the template flush over the square piece and drill the first, outer hole. (All holes are blind holes 1³¹/₃₂ in. deep. Adjust drill press accordingly.) Insert a locking dowel pin into the first hole. It will keep the template from slipping and you may now drill the remaining holes.

Rotate the square piece 90°. Insert a dowel into the first hole on the side. Place the template so the half hole cutout rests on the dowel (see bottom picture). This will offset the template ⁹/₁₆ in. from the end. Drill the holes. If you insert dowels in the holes drilled earlier, before drilling these holes you will also cut out the notch in the dowels.

The next step is to drill the holes for the locking dowel pins. The square piece is rotated again, a dowel inserted into the hole last drilled. The template will now be offset 1⅛ in. Drill the holes for the pin, and the notches in the dowels.

# Chair and Stool

The operation of the drill template has been described. This principle applies to all furniture. Once all the square pieces have been correctly predrilled, mount the horizontal dowels (seen from the front on the chair shown) between the square legs. Check that square elements are parallel! Then redrill the holes again with the ¾ in. bit for the side dowels. This puts a groove into the dowel which has already been inserted, into which the side dowel is inserted to check. The same process is re-

Material required for one stool: square lumber 2³/₁₆" x 2³/₁₆"— 4 pieces 19¾" long; ¾" dowels: 8 pieces 19⅝" and 8 pieces 2⅜"; ¾" plywood: 1 piece 20¹/₁₆" x 20¹/₁₆"; Note: You may wish to use veneer edge tape for finishing edges

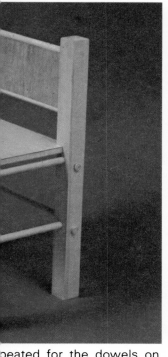

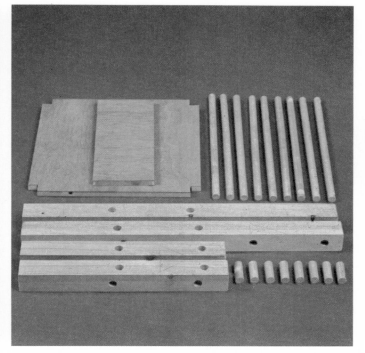

**Material required for one chair:**
Square lumber 2³/₁₆″ x 2³/₁₆″: 2 each 31½″ long and 2 each 19⅝″. Dowels, ¾″: 9 each 19⅝″ and 8 pieces 2⅜″. Plywood, ¾″: 1 each 18⅝″ x 18⅝″ and 1 each 15¹¹/₁₆″ x 6½″.

peated for the dowels on the side of the chair. The locking dowel pin is inserted into the groove of the side dowels. The seats of plywood are first notched at the corners to fit snugly. They rest on the top cross-dowels.

The back of the chair, also made of plywood, is routed at top and bottom edge to a half-round channel (see photo next page, top right) and fits tightly between the dowels.

The two uprights of the chair-back are now assembled. Rebore and insert locking dowel pin.

Assemble front and rear of chair. Rebore in the predrilled holes for the locking dowel pins.

The locking dowel pins are inserted and driven in to a stop with a slight tap of the mallet.

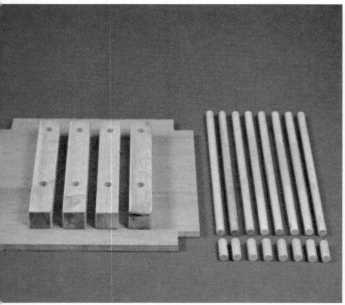

Materials required for this table: 2³/₁₆" x 2³/₁₆"—4 pieces 31½" long; ¾" dowels—8 pieces 35⁷/₁₆" long and 8 pieces 2⅜"; ¾" plywood—1 piece 35⁷/₁₆" x 35⁷/₁₆" and 4 pieces 31½" x 4¾". The plywood for the table skirt must be routed half round.

# Table and Cabinet

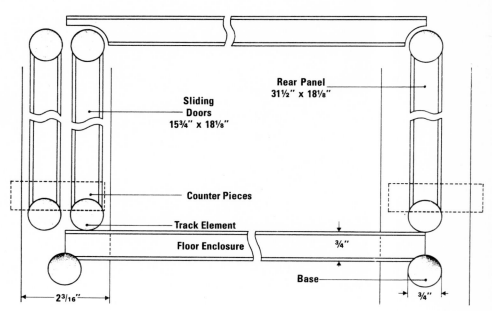

**Sliding Doors** 15¾" x 18⅛"

**Rear Panel** 31½" x 18⅛"

**Counter Pieces**

**Track Element**

**Floor Enclosure**

¾"

**Base**

2³/₁₆"

¾"

These two pieces of furniture are built on the same principle. Both models require cutting a half-round cove for the vertical facings of the table and the sliding doors. For this purpose the drill press can be used with a half-round router attachment or, use a regular router. You can easily see the detailed layout of the dow-

els for the sliding doors of the cabinet in the cross-section drawing through the narrow side of the cabinet.

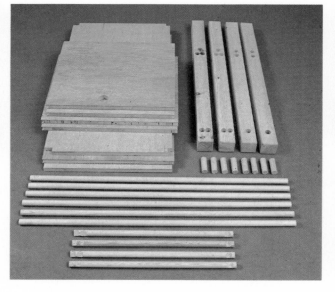

The cabinet doors slide on dowels. Materials required: square lumber 2³/₁₆" x 2³/₁₆"—4 pieces of 31½"; ¾" dowels, 8 pieces 35⁷/₁₆"; 4 pieces, 19¹¹/₁₆"; 8 pieces, 2⅜", ⁵/₁₆" dowels, 4 pieces ¾" long (the purpose of these is not clear—Ed.); ¾" plywood, 2 pieces 17²⁹/₃₂" x 33¾"; 1 piece 19¼" x 31½"; 2 pieces, 15¾" x 19¼"; and 2 pieces 15¾" x 18⅛".

# Easier Furniture Building

Home craftspeople have been wait- 
ing for this: an updated version of the 
time-tested box (or finger) joint. In our 
version the fingers are cut uniformly so 
they mesh, rather than having one 
piece offset as in a ''standard'' box 
joint. In our new application, the joint 
looks completely different, and can be 
made with a handsaw or table saw 
with no great difficulty. If the boards 
you use for the joint are not too thick, 
several can be cut at once.

The joint is suitable for solid lumber 
or for lumber-core plywood. That 
is, the splines that join the fingers can 
be either plywood or solid stock. You 
can save time if you use a wobble 
blade or an adjustable dado blade on 
a table saw. Or, make several passes 
with a standard blade. For this latter 
method you'll need board that acts as a 
spacer fitted against the rip fence; you 
make the first pass, then remove one 
of the boards and make another pass.

Continue until all space boards have 
been removed. The boards are the 
thickness of the spacing for the fingers, so you have automatically cut the 
proper width. Make sure the depth 
of cut is the same as (no more than) 
the thickness of the adjoining piece 
of wood; otherwise the fingers will 
project and have to be sanded flush. 
Height adjustment of the blade is 
critical. ●———→

1

3

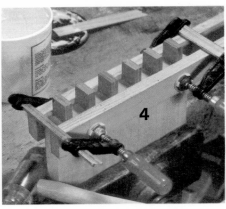

2

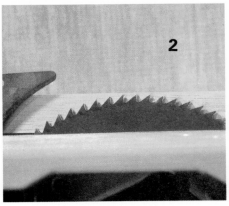

4

1

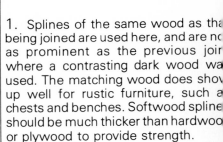

2

## How it's done

1. The glued joint with darker splines can be decorative. If precisely made so the splines fit snugly, and glue is applied carefully, the joint is strong and suitable for the frames of most furniture.
2. Adjust the height of the blade to be the thickness of the stock being used. The advantage of a dado or wobble blade is that every notch and finger will be identical.
3. If the stock being used is not too thick you can clamp several together and cut the notches in one pass. A good idea is to have a block of wood fastened to the face of the miter gauge that is the exact size of the notch. After you make the first notch against the rip fence, you fit the notch over the block, which is spaced away from the blade the width of a finger, then make another pass over the blade. Repeat.
4. To assure that the splines are glued in straight and meet flush, clamp the assembly between two boards. Never tap directly on the splines, use a block of wood between hammer and wood.

## Of Solid Wood

1. Splines of the same wood as tha being joined are used here, and are no as prominent as the previous join where a contrasting dark wood wa used. The matching wood does sho up well for rustic furniture, such a chests and benches. Softwood spline should be much thicker than hardwoo or plywood to provide strength.
2. The splines must not be longe than the wood is thick, which elim nates the need for planing and sandin projecting ends. After the boards a glued and joined, lightly sand the er grain of the splines.

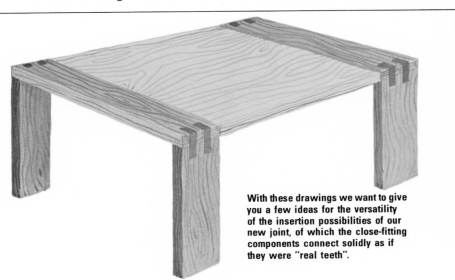

**With these drawings we want to give you a few ideas for the versatility of the insertion possibilities of our new joint, of which the close-fitting components connect solidly as if they were "real teeth".**

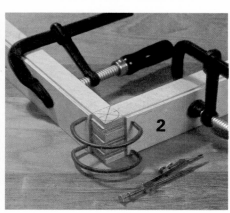

## Lumber-Core Plywood

. Plywood can also be joined with
he splines. The joint will be strong
nough if you space the splines about
in. apart. This assembly method is
xcellent for shelves and cabinets. It is
nportant to apply glue generously to
nd grain, as it soaks up the glue. The
est bet is to apply a coating of glue, let
et a few minutes, apply another coat
ıst before assembly.

. The splines can be cut from
lywood or solid stock of different
nicknesses. Solid stock as thin as
hown is not readily available, so you'll
ave to cut or plane it to suit.

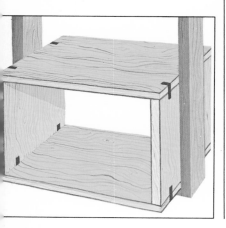

## As a Hinge

1. The splines and modified finger
joint can be used to create a hinge.
Only one side of the splines are glued
to one of the pieces. At the other end,
splines are left free to pivot.

2. After the splines are glued into one
piece, the two pieces are clamped together; the exact center of the corner
is marked and a hole is drilled to accept
a hardwood dowel. Bore holes in scrap
wood to find a bit that will be a snug fit
for a ¼- or 5/16-in. dowel.

3. Double check that both pieces are
in precise alignment, then
use the correct size bit and
drill through the assembly.

4. Clamp parts together
at an exact right angle
after you have inserted
the dowel, then round the
corners of the meeting
splines and fingers. Pivot
the angle in the opposite
direction to permit you to
reach the unfiled and un-
shaped section. Do final
sanding.

5. This is the finished
hinge. The hinge pin may
bind at first, but will loosen
when worked a few
times. A good idea is to
rub some paraffin on the
dowel before insertion.

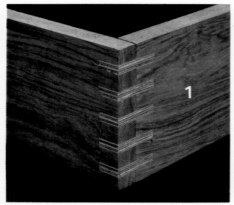

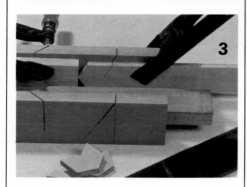

## Not at
## Right Angles

1. Parts that meet at other than a right angle can be joined with the modified finger joint. Hexagons and octagons are assembled in this way.

2. When cutting the notches, be sure that angled ends of the pieces rest solidly on the saw table so the notches are cut the full depth, and correct angle.

3. The arrow-shaped splines are cut from plywood with the aid of a miter box. Cut the arrow shapes a bit oversize, then plane and sand them flush with the surfaces of joined members.

## Very
## Decorative

1. Ordinary laminated plywood makes splines that are extremely attractive, with the several plies showing in strong contrast to the solid lumber. When cutting the plywood splines, use a plywood or planer blade to make sure the plywood does not splinter or chip. Space the splines closely for an especially nice effect—which is ideal on drawers and small chests.

2. Be sure to cut the notches precisely to accept the thickness of the plywood being used. Gaps at the splines weaken the joint, but can be filled with wood filler before finishing.

## Two Types
## of Wood

1. For a strikingly attractive table chest top, join squares or rectangles wood of contrasting colors. T splines are cut from the two woo and alternated for the joints to asse ble the pieces.

2. For the project shown, a number pieces were clamped and glued gether with splines. To ensure that t resulting long strips end up flat a straight, be sure that the pieces clamped to a flat surface until the gl has set. The strips were then edg glued to create a wide piece of sto

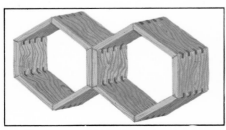

# Creating the Jig
# for a Finger Lap Joint

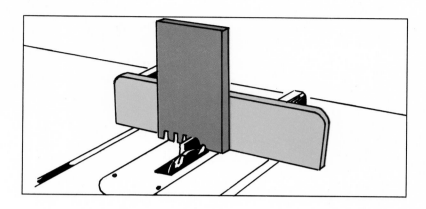

The independent jig is a miter-gauge substitute with twin bars to ride both table slots. Back up the "head" with braces nailed to both the jig and the bars.

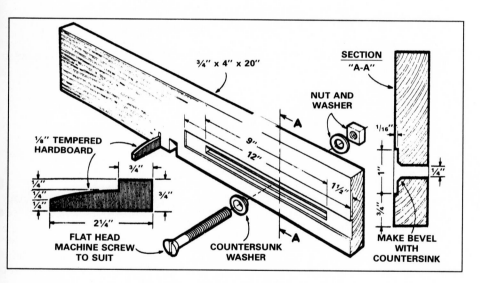

¾" x 4" x 20"

SECTION "A-A"

NUT AND WASHER

⅛" TEMPERED HARDBOARD

¾"

¼"
¼"
¼"

¾"

9"

12"

1½"

2¼"

1/16"

1"

¾"

¼"

FLAT HEAD MACHINE SCREW TO SUIT

COUNTERSUNK WASHER

MAKE BEVEL WITH COUNTERSINK

Adjustable jig provides greater flexibility with finger-lap jointing. Sketch shows details for making this jig.

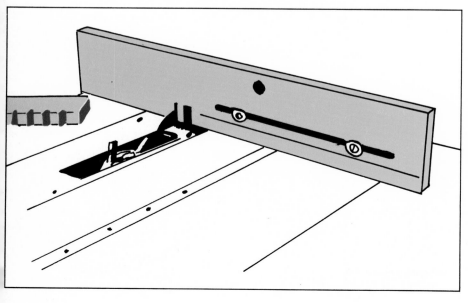

The jig is essentially a piece of 1" stock with cutouts as shown and a piece of ⅛" tempered hardboard as a stop.

# Finger Lap Joint

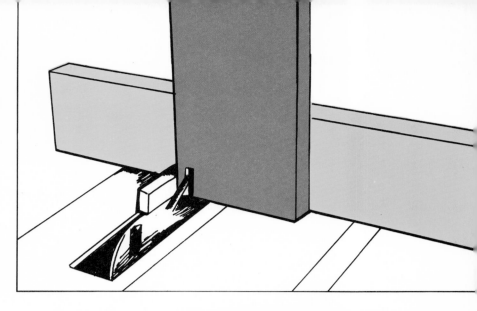

First cut in making the finger lap joint is made by butting one piece against the guide block as you make the first pass.

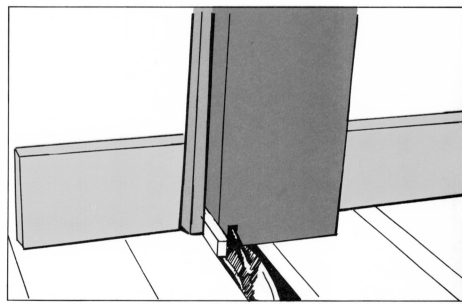

Place the first cut over the guide block and butt the second piece against it. Advance everything to make the second cut.

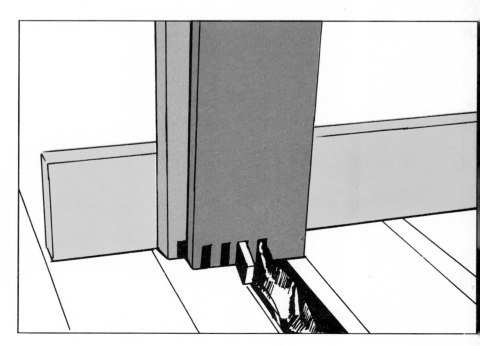

Cuts made are placed over the guide block to position the work for cuts that follow. Throughout the job, be sure that pieces are held firmly together and that passes are made slowly.

# Flower-Power in the living room

With this portable bench you can be sure your plants will be green and blossoming in the right light. Casters make this practical furniture portable, and it could double as a party table.

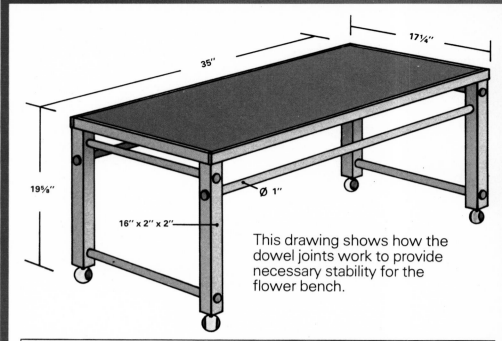

17¼″
35″
19⅝″
Ø 1″
16″ x 2″ x 2″

This drawing shows how the dowel joints work to provide necessary stability for the flower bench.

This flower bench is constructed of dowel rods and square wood. We have used dowels because they are true to size; no other round lumber is manufactured as straight and true to size as dowels. However, there is a disadvantage: dowels 1 in. diameter, as used here, are available only in 36 in. lengths. For this reason the table is 35 in. long. It can be made shorter, but not longer. If possible, purchase lumber cut to the lengths shown in the materials list. Another important note: the edge molding has to be primed and treated with waterproof finish before it is attached with glue, otherwise grout will seep into the wood. Once the molding has been waterproofed, you can glue it onto the edges of the tabletop—first to the longer sides, then to the shorter sides. The molding should be flush at the bottom and raised above the top surface enough so that after the tile is laid it will be flush with the tops of the tiles.

Now drill the dowel holes. First bore vertical holes for each caster, ⅜ in. in diameter, up to the caster stop. Then drill the 1 in. bore holes for the horizontal dowels, according to the drawing. Now apply glue and assemble the base. Avoid excessive gluing.

· We chose 3¼ in. x 3¼ in. tiles for the tabletop; they are available in most tile shops. You can purchase the tiles already adhered to a plastic or net backing, which assures uniform spacing on application. With ¼ in. between tiles, the area covered by each

| MATERIALS | | | | | |
|-----------|-----|----------------------|--------|--------|-----------|
| Part | No. | Material | Length | Width | Thickness |
| Legs | 4 | Beech 2 x 2 | 16″ | | |
| Dowel | 4 | Beech | 36″ | | 1″ |
| Strips (molding) | 4 | Beech | 36″ | 1″ | ¼″ |
| Dowel | 1 | Beech | 36″ | | ⅜″ |
| Tabletop | 1 | Cabinet grade plywood | 35″ | 17¼″ | ¾″ |
| Tiles | 50 | | 3¼″ | 3¼″ | |
| Casters | 4 | | | | |
| Glue | | | | | |
| Grout + Oxide | | | | | |

tile, and surrounding grout, will be 3½ in. x 3½ in. If you decide to use another size of tile, watch the dimensions; the length of the tabletop is 35″, and you must leave space for the crevices.

After adhering tiles, apply grout, which is tinted with iron oxide. Allow to dry slightly; remove excess with a moist sponge, and rub tiles clean with a rag. When the tiles have set firmly, turn the tabletop over, place the leg assembly on top, and mark positions of the legs. The dowel holes are drilled into the tabletop with a spacer (photo 5). Now prime and finish the base and glue on the tabletop. Finish by inserting the casters.

**1. Do not use too much glue: what oozes out will look ugly. Saw spacers from scrap lumber so that all dowels will protrude uniformly.**

# A sturdy dowel joint.

The cutaway models show the principle behind our dowel joint — everything fits tight. Shorten the bottom dowels according to the caster sleeves.

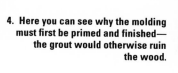

After the base has been assembled, you will have to wait for the glue to harden before drilling through the leg and into the dowel.

3. Gluing the tiles in place is quick and easy, especially if you use tile adhered to a plastic or net backing.

4. Here you can see why the molding must first be primed and finished— the grout would otherwise ruin the wood.

5. The dowel holes are drilled into the tabletop with a spacer. The dowels in the base are left to protrude and are sawed off once glue has dried, which ensures that the peg is no longer than the tabletop thickness.

25

# For Collectors:
# Curio display case

## This coffee table is intriguing; its built-in illumination will place your collection in the right light.

True collectors are especially proud of the most beautiful pieces in their collection. We have invented the ideal storage for collections of particularly small objects . . . a collector's table which can accommodate your entire collection. The best pieces are visible, with the remainder carefully distributed over either 8 or 16 individual drawers. It is far superior to most showcases because it can be illuminated from within by built-in tube lights and in addition serves a practical purpose: we have planned its dimensions to make it suitable for daily use as a coffee table or end table. This table requires a top-notch hobby craftsman.

For reasons of work time . . . and this you will understand from the series of working photographs . . . we show the case built with only 8 drawers; the construction drawing and list of materials, however, provide for 16 drawers in case you wish all of them for your collection. Furniture casters will make the collector's table even more flexible.

In addition we have paid special attention to a solid appearance, because precious things must have a precious frame. Brass pulls on drawers, felt or velvet for underneath the objects, mahogany frame and drawer fronts, as well as Hessian sack cloth wall covering and plate glass, provide this frame.

If our suggested construction is to be an especially successful one for you, precise work . . . particularly for the details . . . is of the utmost importance. Thus, the mahogany frame should be cut only using a mitre box, and care should be taken not to unnecessarily scratch the plexiglass panels when predrilling holes, because damages to the plexiglass are difficult to repair later on. Furthermore, it is very important that all dimensions are followed exactly as indicated, and felt and sack cloth are glued on using only a very thin and even coat of adhesive. A heavy droplet will stain the fabric and cannot be removed afterward.

When you have finished the insert, just place it loosely, otherwise defective lightbulbs cannot be changed later on. In the interest of safety, leave the installation of the lighting fixtures to your electrician.

**Old cigar boxes serve a purpose, but cannot compete with our collector's table, which offers both storage and order.**

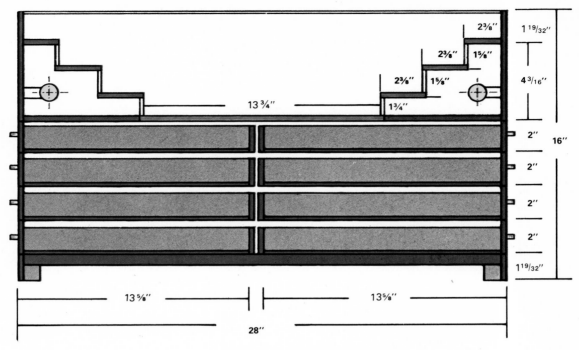

## LIST OF MATERIALS

**Frame pieces**
Mahogany
8 pieces   16″ x 1¹⁹/₃₂″ x ¾″
8 pieces   28″ x 1¹⁹/₃₂″ x ¾″

**Filler Panels**
Pressed wood particleboard
2 pieces   25¹/₂″ x 13¹⁹/₃₂″ x ¼″
2 pieces   25¹/₂″ x 5³/₁₆″ x ¼″

**Center Bottom**
Particleboard
1 piece   26¹/₂″ x 26¹/₂″ x ⅝″

**Center Wall**
Particleboard
1 piece   25″ x 8″ x ⅝″

**Bottom Frame**
Fir
5 pieces   26¹/₂″ x 2″ x 1¹⁹/₃₂″

**Drawers**
Mahogany
16 pieces   12¼″ x 1⅞″ x ¾″
Fir
32 pieces   12⅞″ x 1¾″ x ½″
16 pieces   11 x 1¹³/₃₂″ x ½″
Fiberboard
16 pieces   12⅞″ x 11½″ x ⅛″

**Guide Rails**
Fir
8 pieces   26½″ x ¾″ x ¹³/₃₂″
8 pieces   26½″ x ¼″ x ¹³/₃₂″

**Insert**
Particleboard
1 piece   26½″ x 26½″ x ¼″

**Plexiglass**
2 pieces   21½″ x 2″ x ⅛″
2 pieces   21¾″ x 2″ x ⅛″
2 pieces   16¾″ x 2″ x ⅛″
2 pieces   17″ x 2″ x ⅛″
2 pieces   12¼″ x 2″ x ⅛″
2 pieces   12″ x 2″ x ⅛″

**Additional Supplies**
16 pieces drawer knobs
70 pieces brass screws
24 pieces iron screws
2 running-meters cable
2 pieces sack cloth wall covering
      25¹⁹/₃₂″ x 13¹⁹/₃₂″
2 pieces sack cloth wall covering
      25¹⁹/₃₂″ x 5³/₁₆″
1 piece felt
4 pieces tube lights, 20″ long

**Plate Glass**
1 piece   28″ x 28″ x ¼″

**1.** Mahogany panels form the decorative frame Mitre-cut corners are connected firmly with wooden dowels and glue.

**2.** Using a rubber roller, press the sack cloth onto the ¼ in. thick particleboard side panels which have been evenly coated with glue.

**3.** Using wire nails, fasten covered side panels to mahogany frame.

**4.** The tension necessary to press all side panels together is obtained by means of a clothesline. Angles between side panels must be exactly 90°, use wooden spacers.

**5.** Drawers are glued together. Outer grooves of the side panels must be ¹³/₃₂ in. wider than corresponding guide rails. The bottom is held by inside grooves.

**7.** Fluorescent lights are screwed onto the center plywood floor panel, one in the center of each side. The cable is laid to lead downward through a hole at the edge.

**8.** Spaces are constructed from the individual sections of the ⅛ in. panel and the precut plexiglass panels. Individual sections are connected by brass screws.

**6.** Wooden strips serve as guide rails for the drawers. They, too must be lined up exactly, otherwise drawers will bind. They are fastened simply by means of screws.

# A first car just like dad's

The picture series above speaks for itself. A little tow-head makes her acquaintance with her first car. Steering wheel, controls, accelerator, brakes and seat position are inspected and off we go with a little push from dad. Any child will be delighted with this top-of-the-line model from the family auto plant, and you will have the fun of putting it together.

Our playmobile is constructed of hardwood so that it will not be totaled if Suzy misses the entrance to the garage. Even so, it has everything that is on dad's car: steering wheel, accelerator, controls, brakes, a trunk, and hood with grill. What you will need in materials is given in the sketch on page 32. All yellow parts are ¾ in. (1 in. nominal) thick and all red parts are 1⅛ in. (5/4 in. nominal) thick. The side panels are glued onto the chassis (measurements 23⅝ in. x 23⅝ in. x ¾ in.) and doweled. The tailgate (8²¹/₃₂ in. x 5½ in. x ¾ in.) is fitted to the rear.

This is how the undercarriage looks. No ingenious formula-1-mechanics, but solid axles. A simple and strong construction for drives over sticks and stones.

The completed auto above. Gearshift and brake are easily reached. The trunk space is large and can hold a lot of toys. All connections are glued and doweled.

Dashboard (9¹⁵/₃₂ in. x 5½ in. x ¾ in.) is attached flush against the side pieces. The front seat is installed onto it and has exactly the same measurements as the backrest. The backrest also serves as a handle for you so you won't have any difficulty towing it along.

Drill two holes in the middle of the backrest and saw out a slit. Attach the backrest behind the seat and fasten with dowels onto the side panels. In front of the box, attach the hood. Drill a 1 in. round hole into the upper plate for the steering column. If the drill is long enough, go right through the chassis, since

# The construction of your child's first car is as simple as it is sturdy.

the steering column fits through it also. Now the body is roughly prepared; the only things missing are the moving parts and steering. The wheels are cut with a key hole saw. The diameter of axle holes is 1 in. Attach the rear axle

Teddy bears too can drive this tractor, and your child's friends as well.

bearing in such a way that it is 5⅛ inches from the rear edge. The wheels are fastened on with ⅜ in. dowels. Assemble the front axle as illustrated in the drawing, and tightly glue in the steering column and secure with a dowel pin above the hole in the motor block. Glue on the steering wheel. Attach axle and wheels the same as in the rear. The accelerator has a cut-in honeycomb pattern and a ⅜ in. dowel shaft of round wood. The "gearshift" has two grooves (first and second gear) and is bolted onto the engine block. To finish it off, attach the hand brake.

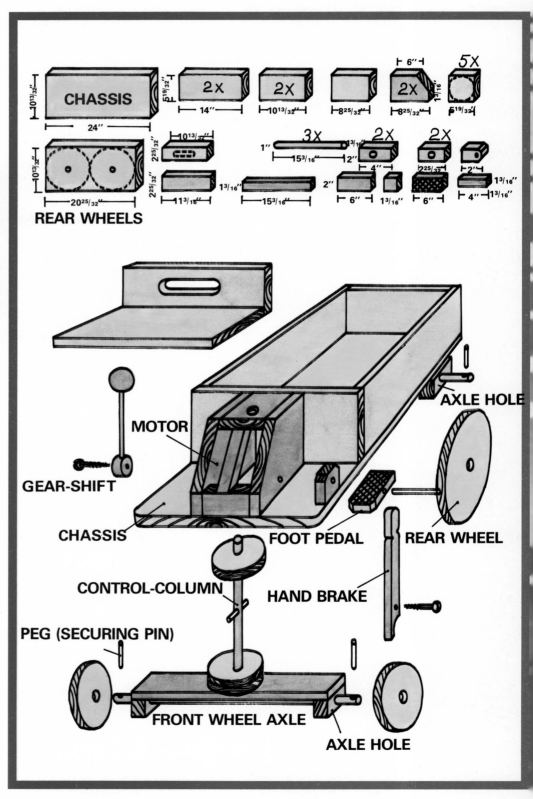

# Bunk-Bed Tower Maximizes Living Space

Two bunk beds, clothes closet, bookshelves, chest and secretary in only 45 square feet! This combination unit makes even the smallest bedroom more livable.

# MATERIALS

**Beds:** 4 pieces 1'' x 10'' x 48''; 4 pieces 1'' x 8'' x 6'6''; If good quality boards are not available, use ¾'' plywood and finish edges with veneer tape.

**Uprights:** 2 x 3 (1½ x 2½); 4 58''; 4 6½''; 26 lineal feet of 1 x 2 for ledgers; 2 pieces of plywood ½'' or more 41'' x 77'' (need not be finished); 8 bed brackets or corner clips; 4 casters.

**Secretary:** 4 butt hinges; 2 flap hinges (on desk); 2 magnetic catches; 2 folding or telescoping hinges; 4 doorknobs; 1 set drawers.

**Clothes Closet:** 2 butt hinges; 2 magnetic catches; 1 closet rod, 24''; 1 doorknob.

**Linen Closet:** 4 butt hinges; 2 magnetic catches; 12 shelf brackets; 2 doorknobs.

**General:** 6 4' x 8' sheets plywood, ½'' or more, surface as desired; 1 4' x 8' ⅛'' or ¼'' hardboard for backs.

**Dowels:** tape veneer; nails, screws, glue; burlap for rear panel.

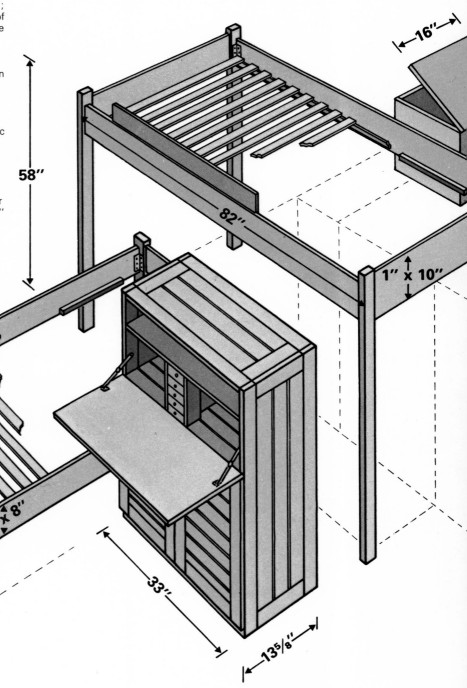

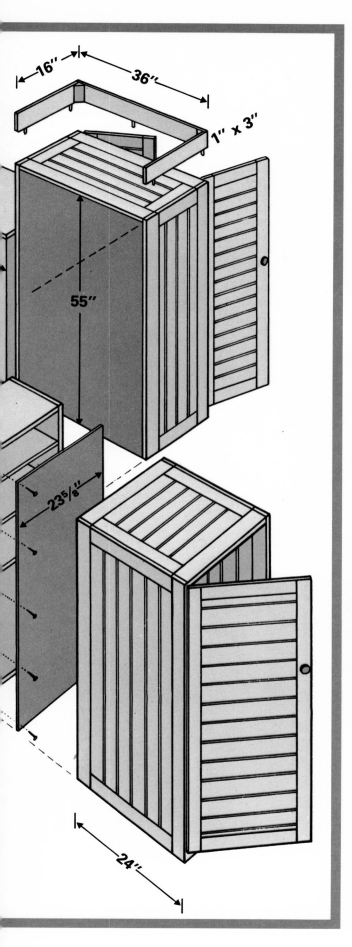

16"

36"

1" x 3"

55"

23⅝"

24"

Toy box and clothes hamper serve as steps to upper bunk.

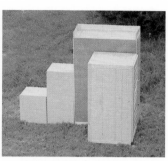

Adding the closet, the tower grows in width.

The bookshelf, with open side toward the bed, is added.

The secretary with bottom cabinet completes the grouping.

One bed is atop the tower. The bottom bed takes its place in the "sleeping hollow."

The materials and components shown here are those used in the original European design. U.S. readers will find it much easier to use patterned plywood instead of the pine tongue-and-groove boards, and bunk beds in the States customarily use a plywood foundation rather than the slats shown.

The U.S. standard bunk bed mattress is 39 in. x 75 in. but you will need 41 in. x 77 in. between sides and ends to facilitate making the bed. Thickness of these mattresses are 6 in. to 8 in. for innerspring, or 5½ in. if polyfoam.

In addition to translating the metric dimensions, we have made adjustments to conform with the above. You may wish to make additional modifications as you build.

For the two beds, start by cutting the bed boards from plywood that is ½ in. or more in thickness; cut to the dimensions of 41 in. x 77 in. This will determine the other dimensions of the bed frame. Allowing an eighth inch each side and end for clearance, the distance between the side rails becomes 41½ in. and the end rails 77¼ in. The lengths of these rails, made of 1 x 8 and 1 x 10, depend on what attachments you use at the posts. They can be mortised or doweled, or take standard bed brackets, or framing clips applied with screws (shown).

Plan on projecting the posts ¾'' toward the outside of the bed. With a dimension of 2½'' on the 2 x 3 posts, this will leave 1'' on the inside of the bed to be notched out of the bed board. The bottom bed rests on casters to facilitate makeup.

Apply 1 x 2 ledgers on the inside bottom of the side rails. Glue and nail.

The steps to the upper bunk consist of two plain plywood boxes. The smaller box can serve as a toy box, the larger one as a laundry hamper. Make these out of ⅝ in. plywood, with corners butt-joined or mitered. If butted, use veneer tape to cover edge grain. Attach covers with hinges or piano hinges, mortised as required.

**Using plywood, the frames may best be mitered rather than doweled as shown.**

Here is a view into the assembly; the optional burlap rear panel is not shown.

The secretary offers sufficient space on the inside for all that is needed in a home office. The stack of drawers is very attractive.

At left: Reverse board and batten planks; we recommend however, that you use particleboard, or plywood to save effort.

The desk top is attached with flap hinges, and hardboard, the remaining doors with butt hinges.

Most English language builders will not have the patience to build the cabinets of patterned boards as shown, preferring instead the use of plywood, particleboard or hardboard, patterned or plain. We leave this choice to you.

The drop-table of the secretary is best made of ⅝'' plywood with a plastic writing surface. In addition to the support of the folding hinges, (or telescoping brackets), it is best to support the door with telescoping 1 x 2's supported on the inside of the cabinet (not shown).

The drawers inside the secretary can be purchased ready-made of either wood or plastic.

# Living room storage wall can move with you

The components of this wall unit are glued together using 6 in. wide boards; wider ones would warp too fast. The shelf boards are ¾ in. x 6 in., and the cabinet boards are 1¼ in. x 6 in. The cabinet floors of the two outer components and of the 20 in.-wide cabinet will be tightly screwed on. The floors (bottom sections) of the third component from the left will be doweled only. For more stability, you may wish also to screw in the shelf-floors that are second from the top. To make that possible, shelves have to be staggered. All the other bottom sections rest on brass supports. These brass supports may not be available in some parts of the U.S.; in that case we suggest standard pilaster strips with clips.

After sizing and gluing the 6 in. pieces to form the sides and bottoms, drill necessary holes for the brass supports. For easy adjustment of the heights of the bottoms and shelves, locate sleeve supports every 4 in. For the upper and lower shelf bottoms, the cabinets will need a ¼ in. groove on their sides.

Since high gloss does not look good on pine, we suggest two applications of a hard clear primer. The wood needs this protective coat against sunlight infiltration that causes color change.

## Wet all surfaces and sand lightly to raise grain

Follow the picture series on next page to assemble the wall unit; if you wish additional stability, you may secure the unit to the wall with small metal support strips.

The 27½ in. high full doors and the 15 in. high flap doors consist of the frames combined with solid-wood center pieces; the frames are glued to-

**This storage wall is built from solid pine. Pine is not too expensive, and is easy to work and finish, but you may wish to substitute plywood for some parts.**

Soak and sand frame pieces and door centers. After working the grooves and rabbets, each pair of frames and door centers can be glued together.

The vertical frame boards should be glued and screwed to cabinet components. Use putty to cover screw holes.

The hinges are not mortised; they are simply screwed on.

To give you variety of different shelf positions, insert sleeves for your bottom supports (or pilaster strips) about every 4'' to 6''.

For better stability, secure the vertical sidewalls to the wall using a few metal strips with screws.

## LIST OF MATERIALS

### Solid pine, ⅞''

| | |
|---|---|
| 5 sides* | 12'' x 78'' |
| 3 sides | 6'' x 27½'' |
| 1 side | 6'' x 43'' |
| 3 sides | 6'' x 15¾'' |
| 8 bottoms* | 17¾'' x 31½'' |
| 2 bottoms* | 17¾'' x 19⅝'' |
| 9 shelf bottoms* | 11¾'' x 31½'' |
| 2 shelf bottoms* | 11¾'' x 19⅝'' |
| 8 door frames | 2¾'' x 30¾'' |
| 2 door frames | 2¾'' x 18⅞'' |
| 4 door frames | 2¾'' x 27½'' |
| 6 door frames | 2¾'' x 14⅞'' |

*finish dimensions, put together with 6-in.-wide boards.

### Solid pine, ⅝''

| | |
|---|---|
| 2 door centers | 27½'' x 22¾'' |
| 2 door centers* | 10⅛'' x 27½'' |
| 1 door center | 10⅛'' x 15¾'' |

### Plywood, ⅝''

| | |
|---|---|
| 6 bottoms | 31½'' x 15⅜'' |
| 1 bottom | 19⅝'' x 15⅜'' |

### Plywood, ¼''

| | |
|---|---|
| 1 rear cover | 84⅞'' x 14⁵/₁₆'' |
| 2 rear covers | 31⅞'' x 26⅛'' |

### Other hardware

10 folding hinges with sufficient screws 5 magnetic catches. Approx. 150 brass support with sleeves (or pilaster strips and clips) ⁵/₃₂'' x 2⅜'' screws.

gether from 6 in. wide boards. The centers will get a 2 in. wide, hollow rabbet all around; in these areas, the wood will be only ⅜ in. thick.

Make a ⅜ in. x ⅜ in. groove in edges of frame parts and key or dowel the corners together. Doors and flap doors are face-attached to your unit (outside edges flush) and therefore should be ¾ in. wider than the opening.

The full doors are flush with bottoms on upper and lower sides; the flap doors are flush on top only, because they require ⅞ in. clearance at the bottom in order to open them. Use folding hinges. To keep doors closed, we recommend magnetic catches.

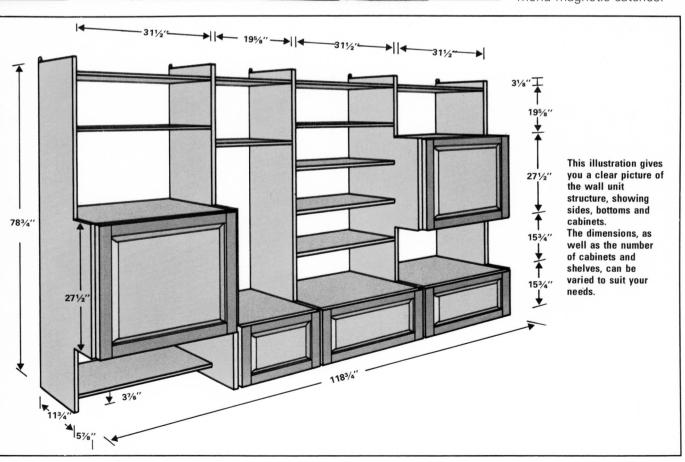

This illustration gives you a clear picture of the wall unit structure, showing sides, bottoms and cabinets.
The dimensions, as well as the number of cabinets and shelves, can be varied to suit your needs.

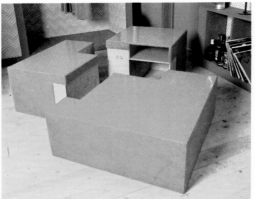

This three-piece table fits into the corner of any cozy seating arrangement. It consists of three units of varying height.

# The Tri-Level Table

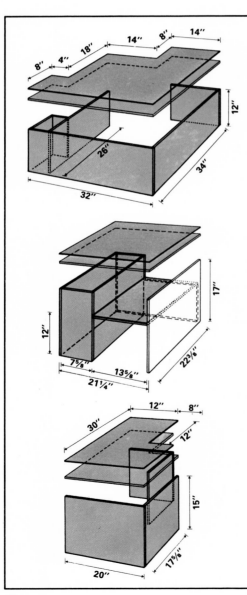

Tinted plexiglass, particleboard, (or plywood) ⅜ in., and carpeting remnants are the basic materials for this table. You can have sheets of particleboard cut to order or cut your own, according to our materials list. The construction is simple: the sections of particleboard are joined with wood screws.

The carpeting remnants are attached to the visible, previously painted top of the table. The effect is even more stunning if the carpeting is the same as that covering the floor: the table then appears to "grow" out of the carpet.

To enhance the color of the plexiglass top, the underlying top of particleboard should be painted. The undercoating should be white for light plexiglass, or black for dark plexiglass.

The individual units (see drawing) are not attached to each other; they are just grouped together.

| MATERIALS | |
|---|---|
| **Top Drawing** | 1 Plexiglass 21¼" x 22⅜" |
| 1   32" x 12" | 1 Plexiglass 13⅝" x 22⅜" |
| 1   33¼" x 12" | |
| 1   26" x 12" | **Bottom Drawing** |
| 1   14" x 12" | 1   20" x 15" |
| 1   7½" x 12" | 1   17⅝" x 15" |
| 1   4" x 12" | 1   12" x 15" |
| 1   32" x 34" Top | 1   11⅝" x 15" |
| 1   32" x 34" Plexiglass | 1   20" x 30" |
| **Middle Drawing** | 1 Plexiglass 20" x 30" |
| 2   22¾" x 17" | **Miscellaneous** |
| 1   20⅞" x 17" | Carpeting remnants, |
| 1   20½" x 17" | adhesive double |
| 1   7⅝" x 17" | face type, |
| 1   13⅝" x 22⅜" | wood screws |

The table for a "young" ho functions are as versati shape is

Child's movie theater

# We have copied an idea which our grandparents enjoyed before us—the home movie theater —so your children can play with it.

"The Miracle Drum," a movie theater made from a cake pan with pictures you draw yourself, is not expensive and the construction is minimal. We have pictured across the top of this page a movie for your "premiere"—scale 1:1— all you have to do is copy it. You can see on page 46 how our "Cinematograph" is assembled. You start with the mirror drum. The mirrors themselves should be made of the thinnest possible mirror glass and should be cut carefully with a glass cutter. Now slip the plywood ring over the tube and glue it to the bottom. Glue the mirror boards to the ring. They will reflect the pictures you have drawn on a strip of paper; insert as shown. A disk (3⅝ in. diameter) is fitted into the center tube at the top and fastened to the top disk in. diameter) with the knob handle. The assembly of the stand is easy: a disk in. diameter) is screwed underneath the picture drum, and a ¼-in.-diameter hole is drilled into the center point of the bottom. The picture drum is fastened to the stand by means of a wood screw. However, this screw should be tightened only enough to permit the drum to turn easily on the underlying disk. Finally, all surfaces are painted a matte-finish white.

The mirror drum. Do not use mirrors that are too thick, because the picture edges will be too obvious. Miter edges of plywood pieces to a 15-degree slant.

The picture drum must not be screwed tightly onto the pedestal. Tighten the screw only enough to allow the picture drum to turn freely.

This is what the children's movie theater looks like before finishing steps. The springform insert is merely seated loosely: there is no need to fasten it with screws.

Once the operator puts the film (drawings on strip) in place, the performance can start. Simply use the knob to turn, and the pictures begin to "move"

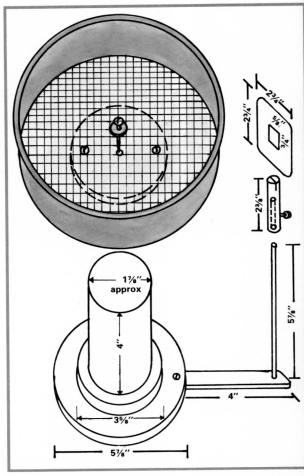

The Mirror Drum. The plywood ring is slipped over the center tube and fastened to the bottom with contact cement. Glue the mirror drum on it and close it with the plywood disk (5" diameter). Fit the ⅝" disk into the tube. Glue both disks together and secure by screwing in wooden knob handle. The mirrors are also fastened with contact cement.

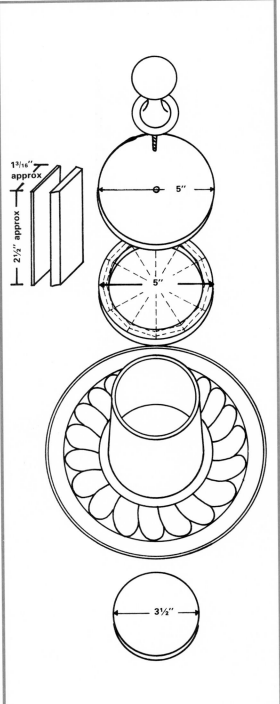

1³/₁₆" approx

2½" approx

5"

5"

3½"

Picture drum, stand and viewing window. The springform cake pan has a diameter of 8¾". Both disks for the stand are made of ½" plywood. Make the viewing window of leftover sheet aluminum, plywood, or stiff cardboard. The strip of wood which carries the viewing window is glued into a notch under the foot of the stand and secured with a screw. Finally, all inside surfaces are painted a matte white.

## MATERIALS

1 cake pan (springform, with tube cake insert), 8⅝" diameter; 12 mirrors, 2½" long, 1³/₁₆" wide—as thin as possible.

| No. of pieces | Material | Length | Width | Thickness |
|---|---|---|---|---|
| 1 | plywood | 20" | 10" | ⅜" |
| 1 | plywood | 10" | 6" | ⅝" |
| 1 | pine | 4" round, diameter 2" | | |
| 1 | hardwood | 6" dowel rod, diameter ¼" | | |
| 1 | hardwood | 2⅜" dowel rod, diameter ⅜" | | |

1 wooden knob handle with wood screw
1 wood screw with washer disk ⅛" x 2"
1 piece sheet aluminum 2¾" x 2¾"
wood glue, contact cement, paint

46

# Conversation Pit for Living or Family Room

The unique feature of this conversation pit is that it can be
built into almost any size room; dimensions can be varied to suit.
The "pit" in the center of the room is created by a platform 7½ in. high.
The various levels and soft velour carpeting transform
an ordinary room into a cozy and comfortable place in the home.
When friends come to listen to the stereo or just to talk,
the platform can be used for additional seating.
TIP: Build in stereo wiring and components.

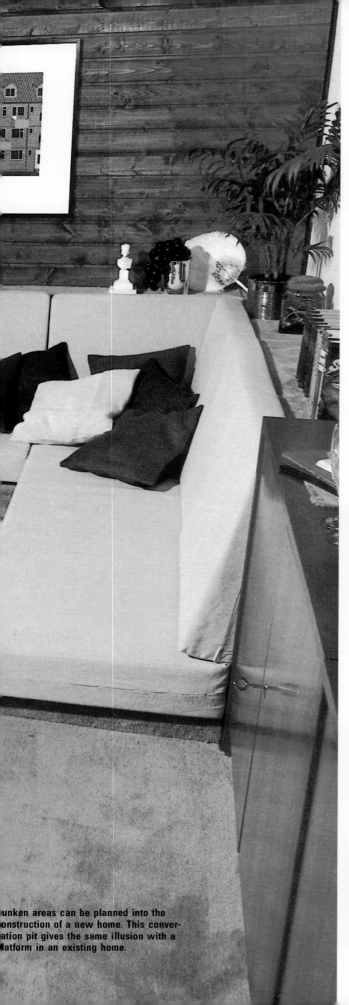

Sunken areas can be planned into the construction of a new home. This conversation pit gives the same illusion with a platform in an existing home.

Part of the charm of this room lies in the varying heights of the components: platform 7½ in.; seats, with 7-in. cushions, 13 in.; and shelf height 33½ in.

You may wish to carpet the entire room before setting up the seating and the platform. This allows the seating to be removed without having to install new carpeting.

The seating is built in three sections: the center (end) section is placed between the two side sections. The platform is placed in front. Steps are used only if needed.

All components are built of ¾-in. particleboard, and are simply glued and screwed together. The carpeting, which is applied with a special adhesive, can be of your choice. Shown is a synthetic velour. Foam rubber pads can be 4 in. to 5 in. and are covered with denim.

First, the slanted back supports are glued and screwed to the crosspieces of the seats (photo 1). Be sure to keep the outside angles at 90° so that all inside angles correspond.

When all pieces have been glued, they can be attached to the base at the front (see sketch). The "angles" are screwed to the base flush at the bottom, which extends a little above the top (photo 2). To reinforce these parts, triangular cant strips are glued

1. The supports of the backrest, already cut at a slant, are glued, then screwed to the crosspieces.

2. Now all angles can be screwed to the front of the base. Countersink screws.

3. Here's a look at the frame for a seat-corner. The top ledge extends about ½" so it can be fitted to the wall.

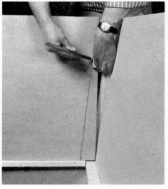

## MATERIALS

¾'' particleboard (unless otherwise indicated), (cut from 4 ft. x 8 ft.)

**Platform**
6¾'' x 61 lineal feet
2½ sheets 4 ft. x 8 ft. for top

**Corner Element**
1 37½'' x 37½'' x ¾'' plywood
2 rear panels ¼'' x 36⅝'' x 26⅜'' plywood
2 sides 10¼'' x 26⅜'' x ¾'' plywood or boards
2 shelves
  1 36⅝'' x 10¼'' x ¾''
  1 26⅜'' x 10¼'' x ¾''
  plywood or boards.
For best appearance, use all same wood and grade for both plywood and boards.

**Seating at Right**
1 base 90'' x 9''
4 crosspieces 36⅝'' x 7½''
3 supports 32¾'' x 10¼''
1 rear panel 82½'' x 24¾''
1 seat 78¾'' x 26⅜''

**Seating at Left**
1 base 115⅛'' x 9'' (since this exceeds the 96'' panel size, you may either splice, or use a 1'' x 10'' x 10'0'' board ripped down)

4 crosspieces 36⅝'' x 7½''
3 supports 32¾'' x 10¼''
1 rear panel 78½'' x 24¾''
1 seat 76⅜'' x 26⅜''

**Center Seating**
1 base 53⅜'' x 9''
3 crosspieces 36⅝'' x 7½''
3 supports 32¾'' x 10¼''
1 rear panel 83¾'' x 24¾''
1 seat 52⅝'' x 26⅜''

**Box**
2 sides 50½'' x 24½''
1 top 50½'' x 17¼''
1 end 26'' x 17¼''

**Foam Padding 4'' to 5''**
7 28'' x 25⅝''
1 25⅝'' x 25⅝''
8 28'' x 18½''
1 23¼'' x 18½''

**Miscellaneous**
60 lineal feet—¾'' x ¾'' or 1'' x 1''
13 lineal feet—1'' x 1'' cant strip (triangular)
30 lineal feet—¾'' x 7½'' particleboard
32 yards carpeting
12 yards denim or other seat covering.

**4.** This shows how to scribe the slant of one back panel to the other. Slide a block of wood along one panel while marking the other.

**5.** After all parts have been assembled, the carpeting can be attached. Use special adhesive.

**6.** To obtain a neat corner, attach carpeting first on one edge and then cut off at 90° angle at the corner.

**7.** This shows how the edge of the carpeting is held in place: screw a wooden ledger against it from the inside; it also supports the seat.

and nailed in the corners.

Now you can screw the back onto the slanted supports. The top edge at the back panel must be beveled with a plane to accommodate the ledge that goes on top, and which is about ½ in. wider than necessary to permit it to be scribed and cut to an irregular wall. This should be done before applying the carpet.

Carpeting can now be glued to the fronts of the base, the back panels and the ledge; prime the particleboard first for better adhesion. Fold the carpeting around the edges to prevent it from coming loose (photos 5 and 6) Inside the base, secure the carpeting with a wooden ledge which also supports the seat. This is ⅝ in. below

the upper edge and extends all around. Build all three seats this way.

The shelving (left rear corner) consists of a tabletop and shelf. Two sides are screwed together with two rear panels, with the top ledge from the seating holding it together. The center shelf is fastened with screws to the back panel from behind. The tabletop rests unattached on the edges of the seating elements and on a ledge attached to the rear panels. This box is screwed between the ends of the seating elements after it has been finished as desired.

Now the platform can be constructed. The drawing shows the layout of the short supporting spacers. The dimension for 16 in. on

**8.** Where the seating elements abut at the corners, a board is screwed in place to prevent movement.

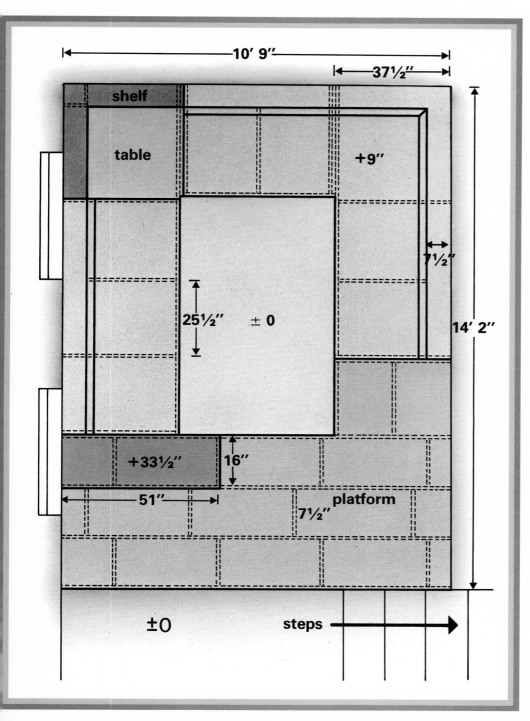

shelf

table

+9″

10′ 9″

37½″

25½″

± 0

7½″

14′ 2″

+33½″

16″

51″

platform

7½″

±0

steps →

center has been adjusted so as to work with standard 4 ft. x 8 ft. particleboard or plywood. Screw all parts together and attach the cover.

The box to the left is made separately and then screwed to the platform. To provide access, leave the front of the box open until fastened. Glue carpeting to the box and the platform.

## The Seating Elements Do Not Have To Be Attached

The table is an open box to which carpeting has been applied on sides and top. The glass is simply placed on top.

Next, cover the seat pads with denim or other fabric. Place the cushions on the seat with the back cushions on top—and your conversation pit is ready.

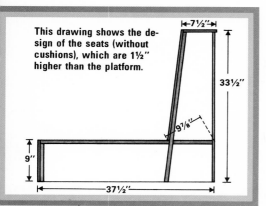

This drawing shows the design of the seats (without cushions), which are 1½″ higher than the platform.

7½″

33½″

9⅞″

9″

37½″

◀ This corner is intended as shelving. The plywood is finished as desired.

Childrens' rooms sometimes look like a battlefield. Paper scraps or other material from the last project, as well as toys, are everywhere. That's when your homemade Mr. Cleanup shows himself to be a true friend and helper.

# Picking up with Mr. Cleanup

## PLASTIC BOWLS:

2 bowls: 12½'' diameter
2 bowls: 8'' diameter
Wood: ⅝'' x 1¼'', length 32''
Plywood: ⅜'' thick 8'' x 12''
5 screws: ¼'' x 1½'' long
1 wood screw: 1½'' long
2 wood screws: 1¼'' long
Plaster, chicken wire, colored jute for hair,
material scraps and plastic glue.

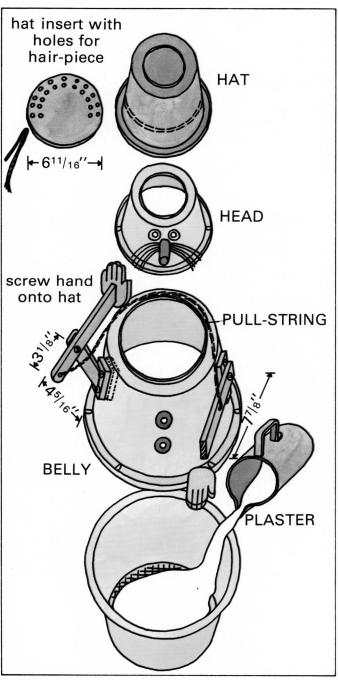

hat insert with holes for hair-piece

HAT

←—6¹¹/₁₆''—→

HEAD

screw hand onto hat

PULL-STRING

←3¹/₈''→

←4⁵/₁₆''→

7⁷/₈''

BELLY

PLASTER

**This detail drawing shows very clearly how our paper-garbage-man is assembled.**

''Hats off'' for paper scraps in the playroom. This funny wastepaperman, made of plastic bowls, helps children pick up messy rooms.

First we glue a disc of chicken wire to the bottom of one of the big bowls (see materials list). Then pour plaster on top of the wire; this gives weight and stability. While the plaster is drying, cut out the bottom of the other big bowl (just inside the rim) and sand the edges with sandpaper. Make the arms, using the ⅝ in. x 1¼ in. wood. First make the arm that lifts the hat. The upper arm is 4⁵/₁₆ in. long and is mitered at 45°, at one end. Glue and dowel the arm onto a 3⅛ in. long piece serving as a support. Attach the 7 in. long lower arm and the plywood hand on the upper arm, using a machine screw as joint. Screw completed arm from the inside onto bowl, by using a counterplate. Attach the 7⅞ in. long stiff arm with two counterplates onto the bowl. The 1½ in. long wood screw is the axle joint for this arm.

Now glue the two bowls together at their rims; use plastic glue. Cut out the bottom of the bowl where the head will be attached. Screw on the nose with moustache from inside. Use jute for the moustache; glue it in little holes that have been drilled in the nose.

The last bowl is the hat, which will be screwed onto the hand of the lower arm. The hat insert, a 6¹¹/₁₆ in. round plywood disc with the jute hairpiece, has to be glued into the hat. Fasten ribbon on hat, attach the pull-string on the arms, and cover arms with sleeves. The mechanism is operated by foot: a round piece of broomstick or dowel attached with strings to the hand will do the job.

This sideboard made of plywood will fit well into your living room or family room. The choice of color is up to you. The veneer can be treated with a colored stain, or painted. A bar and a dinner wagon located in the interior of this furniture piece can be rolled out for convenient service.

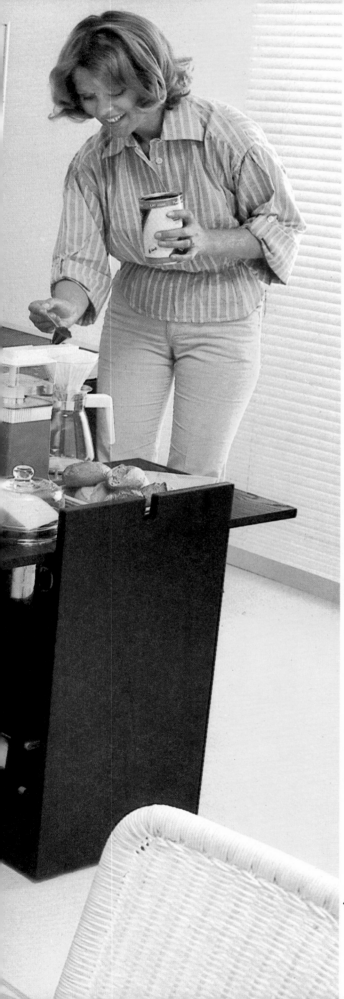

# Sideboard with rolling serving carts

Bar and dinner wagon roll on invisible built-in casters. The dinner wagon is equipped with a rack for bottles and a drawer for drink mixing implements.

◄ The serving wagon's working area is enlarged by two flap-out boards. Divider bottoms create additional storage space.

The three stationary cabinet units are attached to the rear wall panel (shown lying face down) with ¼ in. dowels.

All dowel holes have to be predrilled, and all guide rails for drawers and bottom supports mounted, before gluing side sections to rear wall panel.

Each cabinet unit has a base frame that is ¾ in. in from all four sides. Screw on the base frame strips from underneath.

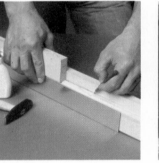

For the table top, lay out and mark off the frame for the inserted veneer top. The aluminum angle molding and top should meet flush. Between top and the aluminum there should be a ¹/₁₆ in. gap.

Miter the aluminum angle. Lay a stiff carton underneath to prevent scratches. Use safety glasses!

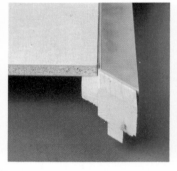

Here you see the top frame with the ¹/₁₆ in. x ¹/₁₆ in. rabbet and the glued-on support strip. The aluminum angle and top are flush, spaced only by the ¹/₁₆ in. rabbet.

After the stain is dry, sand wood against the grain, using a fine grit. Brush the sand off with a brass brush, then apply dull varnish.

Glue mitered aluminum angle with epoxy glue. Clamp until dry. Use wood pieces between clamps and aluminum to prevent scratches.

Polish the aluminum with steel wool. A coat of protective varnish finishes the job.

## Building the sideboard unit

After cutting all veneer panels to size, lay out all dowel holes. All bottom supports or rails for drawers should be attached onto side walls of the unit. The dowels that are 1½ in. long and ¼ in. round are first glued into bottom and side sections of the unit (1⅛ in. deep blind holes). The rear wall has ½ in. deep blind holes.

For your gluing you need two clamps at least 27½ in. long. First glue the bottoms to the side pieces. Once all parts are glued together nice and square, all components will be glued onto the rear wall with the help of the large clamp. Check again for squareness. Next we screw the base under the bottoms. Fit in the doors and drawer front pieces. (Pages 58-59 show how to build the drawers.) Doors are attached with inside hinges. These hinges call for a 1⅜ in. hole on inside of door. Use the same size drill for the pulls in drawers and doors. The holes will then be cut in with a fine saw (see detail drawing same page). Attach moldings to all visible edges.

The picture series on the left shows you how to finish the top piece, which will be glued onto the sideboard unit.

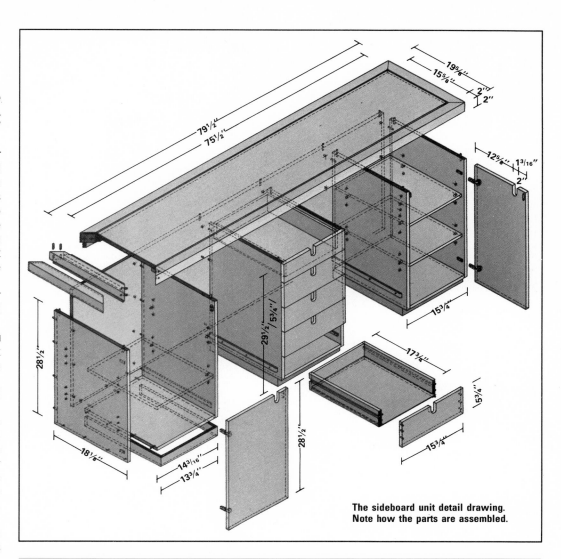

The sideboard unit detail drawing.
Note how the parts are assembled.

## MATERIALS FOR SIDEBOARD UNIT

| | |
|---|---|
| 2 top edging | 2 x 2 x 79½'' |
| 2 top edging | 2 x 2 x 19⅝'' |
| 4 top edging | ¾ x 1¼ x 79½ |
| 4 top edging | ¾ x 1¼ x 19⅝ |
| 1 piece plywood | ¾ x 15⅝ x 75½ |
| 6 sides, plywood | ¾ x 18⅛ x 28½ |
| 1 rear wall, plywood | ¾ x 28½ x 79½ |
| 4 bottoms, plywood | ¾ x 17¾ x 14³/₁₆ |
| 2 doors, plywood | ¾ x 15¾ x 28½ |
| 5 drawer fronts, plywood | ¾ x 5¾ x 15¾ |
| 6 base strips | ¾ x 1 x 17¾ |
| 6 base strips | ¾ x 1 x 15¾ |
| 10 guide rails, beech | ⅜ x ⅝ x 17¾ |
| 5 drawers, wood or plastic | 4¾ x 13¾ x 17¾ |
| 5 drawer bottoms, hardboard | 5¼ x 13 x 17 |
| 2 aluminum angle | 2 x 2 x 78½ |
| 2 aluminum angle | 2 x 2 x 19⅝ |
| 2 magnetic catches | |
| 4 hinges for doors | ¼ x 1½ |
| 56 dowels | |
| 65 flat hd. screws | ³/₁₆ x 2 |
| 25 bottom supports and sleeves | ³/₁₆ x 2 |

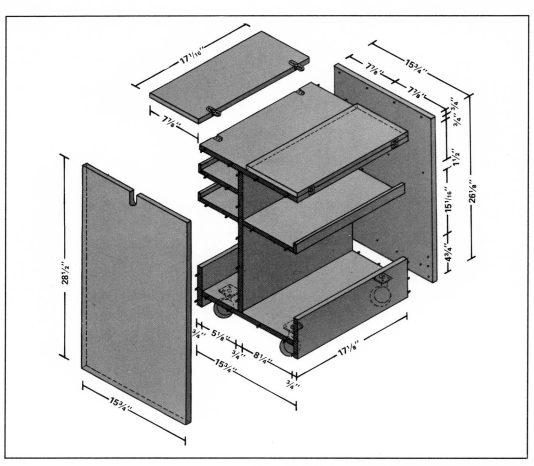

## Serving wagon assembly

If you build the wago[n] in the following order yo[u] should have no problems[.]

The intermediate bo[t]toms are doweled to th[e] vertical center piece. Th[e] bottom piece will be dov[w]eled together with the tw[o] little sideboards. The cas[t]ers are attached usin[g] chrome-plated screw[s.] Glue the center piece ont[o] the bottom, then dowel th[e] working plate onto th[e] center. Always pay atter[n]tion so that all parts glue[d] together will be square t[o] each other, otherwise ther[e] will be trouble when yo[u] dowel the rear wall and a[t]tach the front molding.

**Detail drawing of serving wagon. Use four 180-degree hinges for the table top flaps. The hinges are inserted flush with wood.**

## MATERIALS FOR SERVING WAGON

| | |
|---|---|
| 1 front plywood | ¾ x 15¾ x 28½ |
| 1 rear plywood | ¾ x 15¾ x 26½ |
| 1 top plywood | ¾ x 15¾ x 17⅛ |
| 2 table flaps plywood | ¾ x 7⅞ x 17⅛ |
| 1 lower bottom plywood | ¾ x 14³/₁₆ x 17⅛ |
| 1 center wall plywood | ¾ x 17⅛ x 22⅛ |
| 2 sideboards plywood | ¾ x 4¾ x 17⅛ |
| 2 intermediate bottoms plywood | ¾ x 5½ x 17⅛ |
| 1 intermediate bottom plywood | ¾ x 8⅝ x 17⅛ |
| 3 strips pine | ⅜ x 1½ x 17⅛ |
| 4 casters | |
| 4 chrome plated hinges (invisible) | |
| 12 flat head screws | ⅛ x ⅝ |
| 52 wood dowels | ¼ x 1½ |

**The drawers could be built of hollow channeled plastic material (if available in your store). The corner and dowel components are glued.**

**When the drawer is finished, glue the handle grip and veneer onto the precut pegs.**

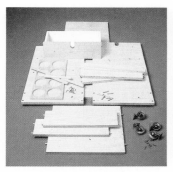

**Here you see all precut parts of the serving wagon. All visible holes are drilled.**

**The centerpiece and all intermediate bottoms are doweled to one sidewall. Then the other side is glued on.**

58

## Bar-container assembly

The assembly of the bar-container is similar to that of the serving wagon. Lay out holes for the bottles with a divider and cut them using a sabre saw. Put putty on the cut edges of holes and sand.

After assembly the barwagon top is flush with the rear wall (which is true also of the serving wagon). In the front the top hangs over 2⅜ in. Once all parts are glued together, check for excessive glue. Sand glue off and stain.

Apply stain as evenly as possible. After assembly, the stained areas receive a coat of semi- or high-gloss varnish. Varnish protects the surface and gives the wood either a duller or higher gloss look (as you prefer).

Application with a spray gun would be the easiest way, but it also can be done with a soft brush.

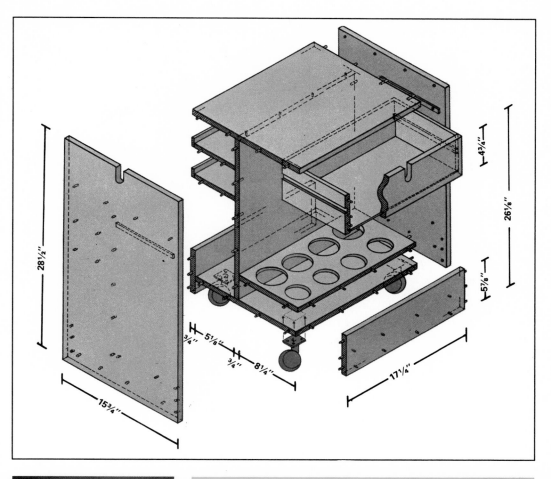

Cut plywood according to dimensions given in detail drawing. The bottom needs a clearance from floor approximately equal to the height of your casters.

Should the plastic drawer material be too expensive, use ¾ in. plywood for the sides, and groove it. Use hardboard for bottoms; glue, and then dowel.

Here is the easiest method. Attach plywood edging with contact cement. Use a half-round tool to rub on trim.

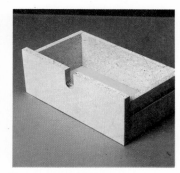

To ensure smooth operation of drawers, machine or saw and chisel a ⅝ in. wide by ⅜ in. deep groove. Use a cutting tool for grooves, or cut in with a saw and chip out with a chisel.

59

# The little engineer:
# Night-express through the Playroom

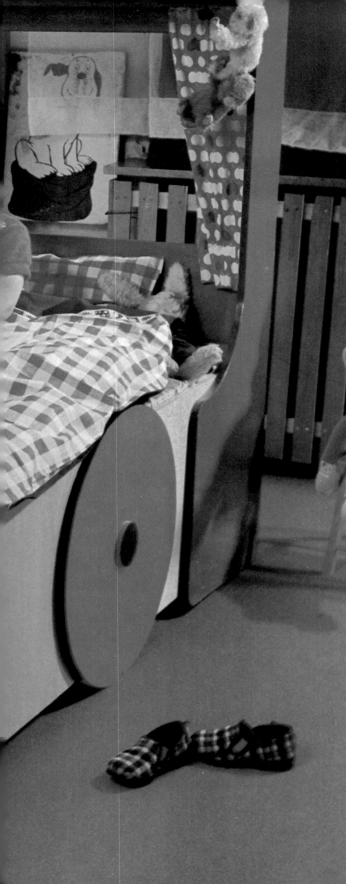

Here's a bed that every child will love, and a toy that you can use not only in the playroom but can also take outside: our juvenile bed-engine which you can build from scratch or around an already-existing bed. A puppet-stage is also included. This piece of furniture has been designed for children aged three to thirteen.

When the crib becomes too small, you begin looking for a bigger bed. The selection is large; however, the solution we introduce is new. Our bed-engine is not only a bed, but a toy and a puppet-stage all in one. The whole bed is made of a varnished sheet of ¾ in. plywood. We didn't give any measurements on purpose, because you can tailor the bed to the age of

your child or the size of the playroom. However, you should remember that the youth-bed should measure at least 55 in. x 27 in.; and, of course, it would be even better to make it twin size. Any desired set of measurements is possible, since you can order foam mattresses to fit.

All parts of the bed are cut out of the plywood with a sabre-saw. Wheels and

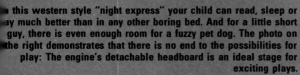

In this western style "night express" your child can read, sleep or play much better than in any other boring bed. And for a little short guy, there is even enough room for a fuzzy pet dog. The photo on the right demonstrates that there is no end to the possibilities for play: The engine's detachable headboard is an ideal stage for exciting plays.

headlights are simply glued to the frame and the front. The detachable headboard is worked in such a way that it can also be used as a puppet stage. Glue and dowel the parts together. Then connect the front and side panels with hinges. This way you can quickly fold the engine up and bring it outside for play. To secure the puppet-stage to the side panels use two thumb screws on each side. You can put the mattress in any way you wish. Install a support board on each side panel for the full length of the bed, then place a box spring or a sheet of plywood below.

Cut all parts of the bed from your sheet of ¾" plywood, using a sabre-saw. You can select your own dimensions, but keep in mind that the puppet-stage has to be at least 55" high to have enough room to play.

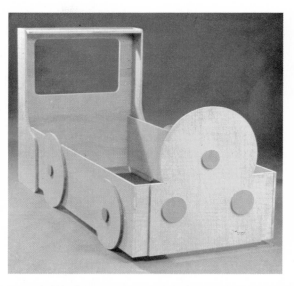

The engine is assembled; simply glue the wheels on the side. The headlights and the rail buffers will be glued on. Glue and dowel the head section and attach to the bed sides with two thumb screws.

We used heavy-duty hinges for the front and side panels, so that you won't have any problem carrying it outside in the summertime. We also recommend a good weatherproof lacquer.

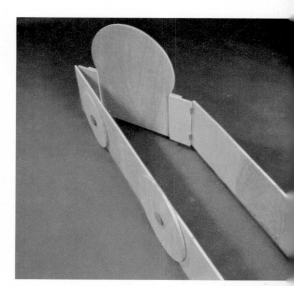

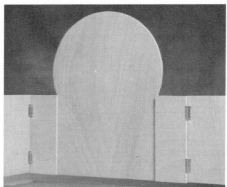

Here you can see very clearly that the front is glued on top of two smaller pieces, which are connected to the sides.

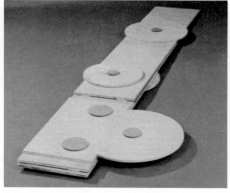

It is simple to fold up front and side panels. When your child gets bigger, the bed can be folded and stored without taking up much room.

The puppet-stage (or headboard of the bed) is detachable.

# A practical bed for your guests

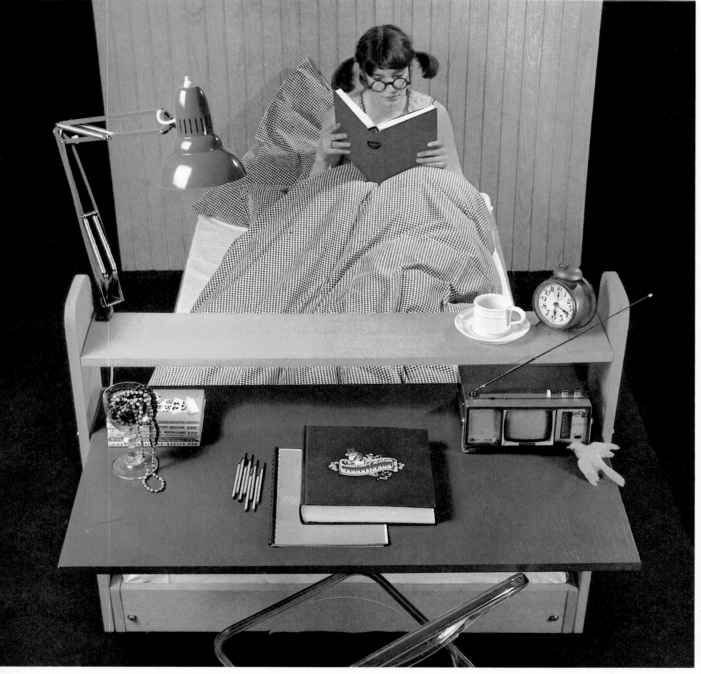

This guest bed is more than just a bed: it combines with a folding desk top to eliminate the need for a storage shelf at the head end. Thanks to the simple peg joints, this bed is easy to build and easy to set up when company arrives. The blue top offers an attractive contrast to the yellow stain of the bedframe, but you can change the color to suit your room decor.

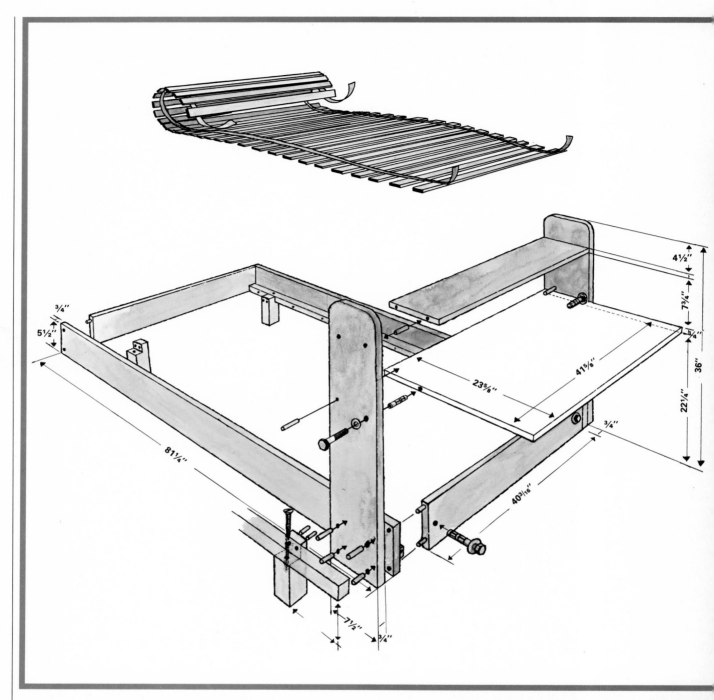

If you take a close look at the drawing, you will see how easy it is to build the bed. Most beds in guest rooms are too narrow and too short; this one is long enough for even a "long" guest to sleep in. The mattress is in two pieces, each one 47¼ in. x 39⅜ in. This is a European size (1200 x 1000 mm); before building the bed check to see if you can buy 4½ in. or 5 in. foam in this size. If not, dimensions should be adjusted to fit available foam mattress sizes. The drawing shows clearly the simple peg assembly; the anchors at the head- and foot-end hold the bed frame together. The two anchors on which the folding desk top pivots also hold the sides, with the shelf between them to the bed frame.

## MATERIALS

| | |
|---|---|
| 2 bed sides | 1'' x 6'' x 81¼'' |
| 2 bed ends | 1'' x 6'' x 40³/₁₆'' |
| 2 uprights | 1'' x 8'' x 35⁷/₁₆'' |
| 1 shelf | 1'' x 8'' x 41¹⁵/₁₆'' |
| 2 ledgers | 2'' x 2'' x 79⁹/₁₆'' |
| 1 desk top | ¾'' plywood 41⅝'' x 23⅝'' |

(or buy prefinished in plastic laminate from a kitchen cabinet shop)
20 slats       ⅜'' x 1½'' (approx.) x 40⁵/₃₂''
6 anchor bolts with expansion sleeve
1 foam mattress, covered, finished size 78¾'' x 39⅜'' x 4²³/₃₂''

Start construction by gluing and screwing the 2 in. x 2 in. ledgers to the long sides. They must be recessed at each end by the thickness of the pine boards. The long sides are then doweled to the endboards (apply glue in the endboard only). Then screw anchors with expansion shields through the endboards into the end grain of the ledgers.

Rabbet the legs on one side and attach the ledger with two dowels. Turn a screw from above into the end grain through the ledger to keep the legs from tilting. Bevel bottom edges of legs with a plane.

The vertical sides for the shelf are attached to the sides of the bed frame with four dowels each (apply glue in the vertical sides only). Dowel the shelf between the sides. Drill a hole in the shelf for the pivoting attachment of the tabletop; also drill a hole into the tabletop after the edges have been veneered. Here, too, an anchor with expansion shield becomes the connecting link. Now hold the tabletop horizontal and mark the hole for the dowel that is located above the tabletop, which will hold it in place when folded upwards.

The slats of the bed are of flexible hardwood. They are held together with strips of webbing that are stapled to the slats.

The tabletop has to be sanded, primed and finished, or covered with plastic. Round all other parts at the edges, pre-sand and then wet all parts with a sponge. Once pieces are dry, finish sanding with fine grit sandpaper. Then you can stain, prime, and finish.

**1.** The side boards are attached to the end boards with wooden dowels. Anchors with expansion sleeve hold the joints. When the screws are turned, they firmly wedge into the wood.

**3.** The slats are connected with a strip of webbing. This can easily be done with a stapler. A piece of scrap of the same slat serves as a spacer.

**4.** Prior to the staining, wet and sand thoroughly. Change the sandpaper often, so that the pores of the wood are not just being compressed. Apply the stain generously with brush or sponge and allow to set briefly. Then rub well, so the stain will dry to an even color. If you do not like the original color-tone, stains of the same type can be mixed.

**2.** The legs are rabetted to fit exactly over the ledger that has been glued to the sides. For proper fit of the slats they may not protrude at the top. They are attached from inside with two dowels (do not glue!), while a screw is screwed from above through the ledger into the end grain. This prevents the legs from tilting under load.

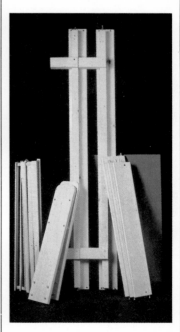

**5.** This bed has another advantage: it can be taken down quickly once a guest leaves, and the space can be used for something else. The parts do not take much room when disassembled. The largest part, the slats, can be rolled up tightly. Of course the bed can also be set up without the folding table. You may wish to use the two pieces of mattress as floor cushions.

This cozy seating arrangement can be built easily and quickly. The basic material—hardwood dowels or a closet pole, preferably 1¼ in. diameter—can be purchased in your local home center. The simple, uncomplicated design of this furniture offers rugged seating at an affordable price for even the inexperienced homeworker.

Both the chair and the settee are o the same construction, so we will de scribe the steps for the chair only.

The dowels are cut to lengths show in the drawing on page 68. The holes fo the ⅜ in. x 2¼ in. locking dowels ar best drilled by clamping the dowels to piece of plywood and drilling them wit a portable electric drill. This piece c plywood can also be used to assembl the sides. (Note: if you have just a ¼ ir drill, it's OK to change to ¼ in. dowels It will be easier if the clamped ends c the dowels are spaced away from th plywood with 4 x 4 blocks for drillin assembly.

# Settee and Chair of Wood and Sisal Cord

About 132' of sisal cord, the size of a clothesline, is enough for stringing the seat of one chair. This sisal cord is often used in macrame work. Windings are spaced about 1¼" apart.

The only decoration on the seating elements: the dowels are wrapped with rattan at the joints (far left). Simply knot the sisal cord at the beginning and the end (left).

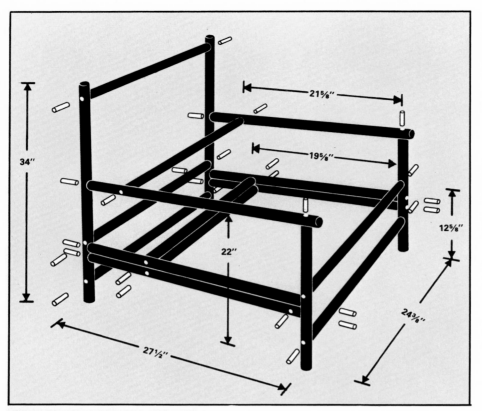

The dowels are inserted with glue and the side of the frame is removed from the plywood only after the glue has set. Then assemble the second side. Dowel and glue the cross members between the finished sides.

The frame of the chair should sit for a day to allow the glue to harden. Then any gaps in the dowel holes may be filled with plastic wood and sanded.

The decorative rattan wrapping—flat 1/16 in. or 3/32 in.—should be well soaked in water to make it pliable and keep it from breaking. At each joint wrap about six 4¾ in. lengths of rattan tightly around both dowels and attach them individually. A longer piece of rattan is then wrapped tightly around the six small pieces and the end is attached.

The finished frame is stained or painted with a satin finish.

String the sisal and install the cushions.

The settee is constructed just like the chair. The front, weight-bearing dowel of the seat and the top dowel of the backrest should be of one piece for rigidity. Cushions are unattached.

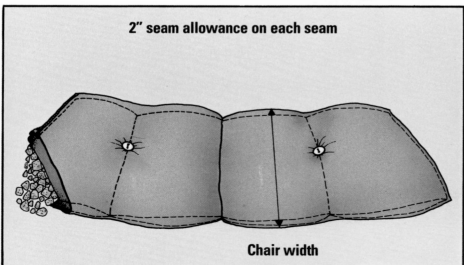

**2" seam allowance on each seam**

**Chair width**

The cushions consist of ticking and a cover of hard-wearing cotton. The ticking, cut corresponding to the size of the seat plus the backrest (don't forget to allow for seams) is stitched three times across its width. This results in four pockets, which are stuffed with foam flakes.
The cover is cut about 8" shorter than the ticking, as the cross-seams are not needed. The cover is attached to the ticking with buttons covered in the same material. A zipper at one end enables you to remove the cover for cleaning.

# A Cabinet with a Twist

This tower of swivel-boxes requires little space and provides a lot of storage. Build this cabinet without sides and guide rails; the boxes swivel to the side to open.

This swivel-box tower is 36 in. high with a base 13 in. x 13 in. It must be attached to the wall, so it will not topple when several boxes are swiveled sideways.

First build the outer U-shaped stand. The rear panel consists of plywood, because it is sturdier than particleboard. Glue and screw strips ¾ in. x ¾ in. to the rear panel flush against the short sides. These strips reduce the lever action of the horizontal top and bottom. They may not be more than 11 in. long, to allow the sides of the top as well as of the bottom box to rest flush against the rear panel. The top and bottom, which are ¾ in. thick, may now be glued in place and secured with screws. Be careful to achieve right angles.

## Butt-Join the Boxes With Screws

The base (see materials list) is built of four parts. It is reinforced by solid wood blocks in all four corners. Glue small strips of wood, flush with the upper edge, to the inside for screwing the base under the bottom.

Now the boxes can be built: two of them are identical. The rear panels of the top and bottom boxes are each recessed by ¾ in. The rear panels of the two center boxes fit flush between the two sides.

This is how the boxes are assembled:

First screw the two sides to the bottom, then attach the front and rear panels between the sides. Then attach the hinges. They are spaced ⅝ in. from the top and bottom edge of the boxes. Mortise for the hinge, plus ½ the diameter of the hinge pin sleeve, into the particleboard. Otherwise there will be too much clearance between box and rear panel. Place the assembled boxes on the rear panel. For even spacing, insert a 1/16 in. spacer between the boxes. Now place the eight hinges not yet attached into the recesses, and mark the lines on the edge of the rear panel, with a square. Now carefully chisel mortises for the hinges. The hinges are attached to the rear panels with screws.

Prior to painting, attach the boxes and check if they swivel without touching.

Set magnetic catches into the rear panel with a drill and screw the counter-plates to the boxes.

Fill and round off all edges.

About ½ in. from the edge, screw the vertical strips (not shown) to the rear panel. They begin at the level of the existing baseboard. These strips can be scribed to compensate for unevenness in the wall.

Now all parts are ready to be primed, sanded and finished.

 The rear panels of the top and the bottom box are recessed by ¾" so these boxes will abut flush against the rear of the stand.

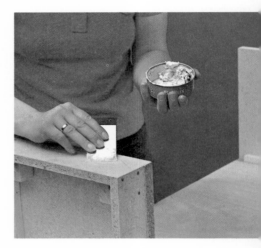

 All edges of the particleboard have to be well filled with synthetic resin filler, so that they will not show on the painted surface.

 Cut mortise for hinges sufficiently deep for hinge pin sleeve to fit. Otherwise, too much clearance will be left between box and rear panel of the stand.

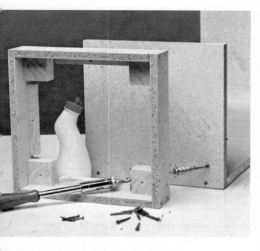

**2**

Reinforce sub-base with blocks of solid wood. Screw base under bottom through ledgers attached on the inside.

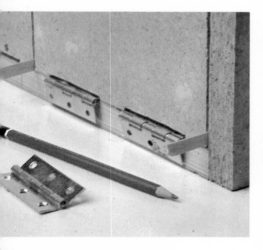

**3**

The hinges are first screwed to the boxes. They are then placed on the rear panel so you will be able to mark their positions.

**4**

Small round magnetic catches, set into rear panel with a drill, keep the boxes from opening by themselves.

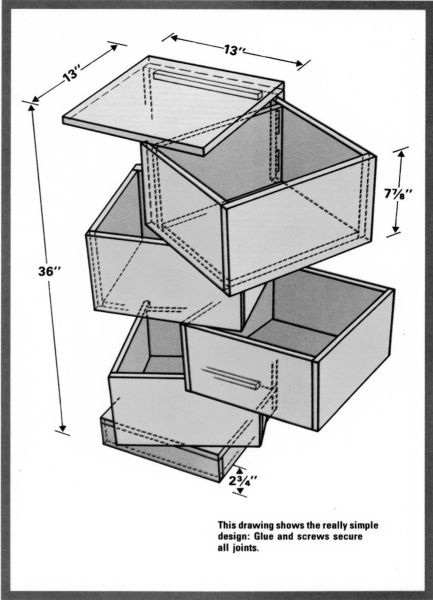

13''

13''

7⅞''

36''

2¾''

This drawing shows the really simple design: Glue and screws secure all joints.

## MATERIALS

**¾'' Plywood**

1 rear panel 31¾'' x 13''

**Particleboard**
2 Tops and bottoms ¾'' x 13''
8 Sides ⅝'' x 7⅞'' x 11⅝''
4 Fronts ⅝'' x 13'' x 7⅞''
4 Rear panels ⅝'' x 7⅞'' x 11¾''
2 Bottoms ⅝'' x 11¾'' x 11''
2 Bottoms ⅝'' x 11¾'' x 10¼''
2 Sides for sub-base ⅝'' x 2¾'' x 13''
2 Sides for sub-base ⅝'' x 2¾'' x 11¾''
10 linear feet of ¾'' x ¾'' pine
8 hinges
24 1'' Screws
100-1⅜'' Screws
4 Magnetic catches

# TIP

To make the swivel box tower mobile, you need four casters and a suitable weight (slab of stone or lead) to be attached to the base. When all four boxes are swiveled out simultaneously, this weight will act as a counterweight. Without ballast, the stack would tip over.

Furniture for people who are flexible.
Bed and benches are not attached,
and can therefore be regrouped
according to need or whim.

# A roomful of furniture for $240

This furniture of pine boards is just right for those who do not want to spend a lot of money and can build their own.

Furniture today no longer has to consist of valuable antiques or heirlooms. Young people particularly, who are just beginning to furnish an apartment, often have to be frugal but still desire an attractive and comfortable home.

Our suggestions will furnish a living room comfortably. When moving to larger housing, the individual pieces can meet needs in other rooms instead.

This set consists of bed, hassock, table, floor-to-ceiling shelving, and two seating benches that also serve as storage space. Apart from minor variations, the construction of all these units is alike. The dimensions, which can be adapted depending upon requirements, can be seen in the list of materials.

We chose 1 x 6 pine (¾ in. x 5½ in.) for the sides. The boards can be purchased eight feet long or longer. First, all long edges of the boards are chamfered. Then the baseboards can be attached with screws (photo 1).

Lay the long boards side by side and drill, using a template. Attach corner blocking strips with threaded bolts. Now position the boards on the short end boards and drill staggered holes (photo 2 and 3).

Before the long benches are assembled, the finger-holes have to be sawn out 1⅝ in. deep and 2⅜ in. wide, so that the covers can be lifted easily (photo 4). They should be centered between three vertical strips. Sand finger-holes well. On the bench with attached shelf the screws are spaced from right to left: at 39⅜ in., 27⁹/₁₆ in., 27⁹/₁₆ in., 23¹⁹/₃₂ in. On the other bench they are spaced 31½ in. apart.

The ledgers for the covers are screwed between the vertical strips. The ledgers are ⅝ in. below the upper edge of the benches, and 2⅜ in. below the upper edge of bed and hassock. To prevent warping, braces are nailed to the vertical strips with overlap (photo 5). They must be flush with the ledgers, and are notched at the corners and the vertical strips for accurate fit.

The vertical posts for the shelf-unit serve also as corner and support strips at the right side of the second bench. The shelf unit is held together by the top and center shelves, which are attached on offset slotted head screws (photos 12 and 13). Glue pine veneer to the shelf edges. Be sure that all corners are notched to receive the 2 in. x 2 in. uprights (check lumber for exact width).

**1.** 1" x 2" or 1" x 3" boards are screwed to the bottom of the lower boards with 1³/₁₆" protruding as base. First apply a few drops of glue.

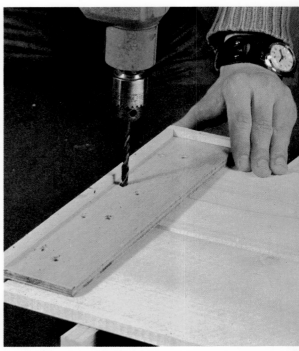

**2.** For uniform spacing of screws, it is necessary to make a drill templ[...] The holes are staggered to avoid the screws coming in contact at t[...] corners. The corner strip is clamped to the boards, drilled, and then [...] attached with screws.

## MATERIALS

**Bed** (41¹¹/₃₂" x 80²³/₃₂" x 12¹⁹/₃₂" high): 4—1 x 6 80²³/₃₂"; 4—1 x 6 39²⁷/₃₂"; 1 bottom ⅝" particleboard 39²⁷/₃₂" x 79⁷/₃₂" (check dimensions); 20 slats—⅜" or ½" x 1½" ± 39²⁷/₃₂"; (use resilient hardwood); 1 foam rubber mattress 4½-5" thick 39⅜" x 78¾".

**Hassock** (23⅝" x 23⅝" x 12¹⁹/₃₂"): 4—1 x 6 23⅝"; 4—1 x 6 22⅛"; 2—⅝" particleboard bottoms 22⅛" x 22⅛"; 1—foam rubber cushion 4½-5" thick; 1—fabric covered 23⅝" x 23⅝".

**Shelf Unit** (Height of room x 41" x 22"): 4—uprights 2 x 2 x room height; 6—shelves ¾" plywood 39¼" x 21"; Veneer edge tape; Pilaster strips and clips, if desired. Bench without Shelving (10'9" x 22⅛" x 12½"); 4—1 x 6 (¾" x 5½") 10'8½"; 4—1 x 6 22⅛".

| | | |
|---|---|---|
| 1 bottom | ⅝" particleboard | 10'7" x 22⅛"; |
| 2 covers | ¾" plywood | 32" x 22⅛" |
| 2 covers | ¾" plywood | 32½" x 22⅛" |

**Bench with Shelving** (10' x 23⅝" x 12½"): 4—1" x 6" x 9'11⅜"; 4—22⅛"

| | | |
|---|---|---|
| 1 bottom | ⅝" particleboard | 9'9⅞" x 22⅛" |
| 2 covers | ¾" plywood | 27½" x 22⅛"* |
| 1 cover | ¾" plywood | 22⅞" x 22⅛"* |
| 1 cover | ¾" plywood | 39⅞" x 22⅛"* |

*Finished size, including carpeting

**Table** (31½" x 23⅝" x 12½"): 4—1 x 6 31½"; 4—1 x 6 22⅛"; 1—⅝" particleboard bottom 30" x 22⅛"; 1—glass top ⅜" x 30" x 22" (check dimensions before ordering).

**Miscellaneous** (for all of the above): 158 lin. ft. 1 x 2, as required; 22 lin. ft. 1 x 1 for corners; 184 ¼" x 2" blued carriage bolts and nuts; 24 ¼" x 3" blued carriage bolts and nuts.

**5.** The horizontal ledgers, which have been screwed to the inside, support the ¾" covers. Nail cross-pieces to the vertical strips to prevent sides from warping. The ⅝" or 1¼" bottom rests on the base.

**4.** Drill corners of the finger holes with the wood bit, then cut with a saw. The remainder is chiseled off neatly.

. Lay long side flush onto short end, apply the drill template, and
re through. For the screw heads to be seated flush against the wood, the
ill must be applied at a perfect right angle. Use a second row of holes
r this job.

Attach the carpeting to the seats
ith a stapler.

At the upper corners of bed
d hassock the threaded bolts are
ained by short metal angles.

**8.** All bottoms must be notched at the corners to fit over the corner strips. The cover board of the hassock, which supports the foam padding, has a 1¼″ hole to ease removal.

**9.** The bed has a bottom like all the other units, which makes this space also available for storage. The base for the mattress consists of slats that can be rolled up. Webbing connects the individual slats.

75

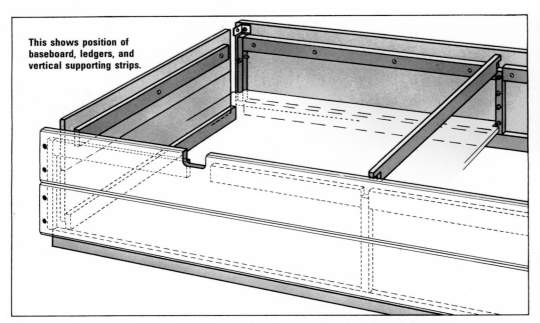

This shows position of baseboard, ledgers, and vertical supporting strips.

**12.** Two shelves are held by offs slotted head screws, which are se into the frame with small expansio shields for greater stability.

**10.** The table does not have ledgers for the ⅜" glass plate. It rests securely on four felt-covered casters hammered into the end grain of the corner strips.

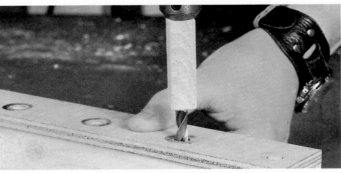

**11.** Holes are drilled 2⅜" apart into the vertical shelf supports to make the shelves adjustable. A drill template is especially important for this job to ensure uniform spacing. Work with a depth gauge if no drill stand is available, or use U.S. style pilaster strips.

**13.** Top: Bore shelves to fit the offset slotted head screws. Bottom The other shelves rest on wooden dowels. All corners must be notche for fit.

The table also has a unattached bottom. Thi creates an attractive, dus free display area. Saw finger-hole into the side t make the glass top remov able. For the bench yo would cover seats wit carpeting (photo 6).

Prime and finish th shelves. All wooden com ponents of the units need final coat of clear finish

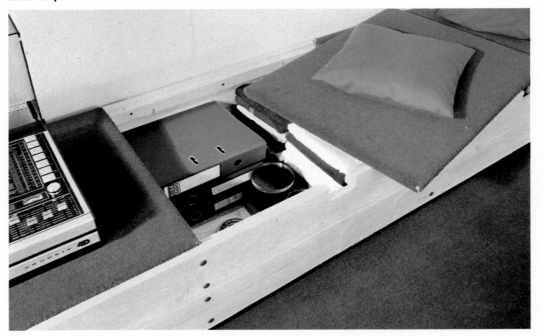

**14.** The long benches are covered in four sections to make storage space more accessible. Individual covers can be lifted using the finger-holes. For greater stability, the bottom should consist of one piece.

# A children's table with muscles

A work table that can withstand rough play. With a sturdy
"muscle-man" on each end, this table can take hammering,
pounding, painting, and scratching without damage;
children will like it at once.

Scrap lumber for nose and moustache, dowel or checkers slices for eyes, and paint: The face is complete.

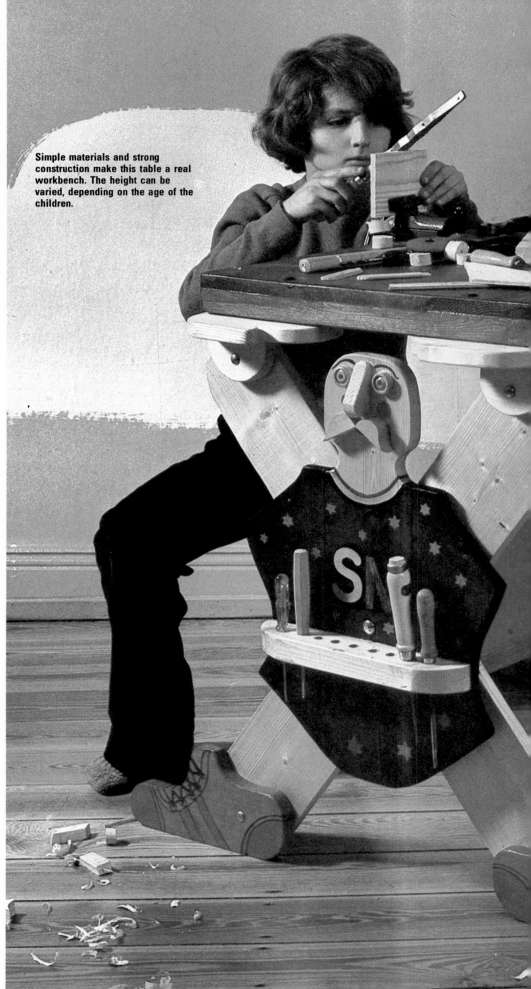

Simple materials and strong construction make this table a real workbench. The height can be varied, depending on the age of the children.

Use smooth dry boards. The drawings show the 22½ in. x 31½ in. table top made from three boards glued and doweled together, but we think ¾ in. plywood is just as suitable, and simpler. Feet, hands and hand braces, as well as boards for the shape of "body" and the "belt", are sawn out with a jig saw according to the layout on the top of page 80 (dotted lines). Smooth all edges with a wood rasp and sandpaper. The legs are rounded off at the ends with a saw. The same is true of materials for the two bodies.

After cutting and smoothing, dowel (or screw) and glue one pair of the four leg boards to the two box sides and attach the bottom; the sides and bottom should already be stained and finished. See exploded drawing on page

**An added feature: The "belt" holds tools in holes drilled in various sizes.**

**Feet in tennis shoes: The football shoes bolted to the legs provide additional support and stability.**

80. On this drawing and in the photo above it, you will see how the hand supports and hands are joined with stove bolts and glue. The holes for the bolts fastening the hands to the table top are drilled about 2⅜ in. from the outer edge of the thumb, but check for exact location after the hands have been bolted to the legs.

Painting colored parts is simple: Use wood stain for the basic colors and latex paints for the decorative elements. Finish with an application of varnish or polyurethane. Drive brass upholstery tacks into the center of each star as decoration. Note: Prior to painting the body, apply sealer to faces and "belt" to prevent staining.

Drill legs on center with a ¼ in. bit, also drill the body on center, about ¾ in. up from the belt. Now bolt

79

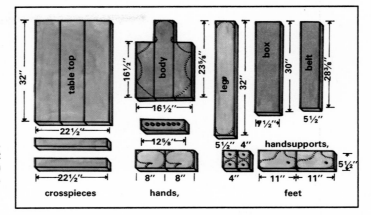

This is the material for the table. The dotted lines show where to cut with the jig saw in order to form the desired shapes.

The basic material for our work table consists of boards of equal thickness in two widths, lath, dowels, and carriage bolts with washers and nuts.

This is how the components look, already doweled and glued, as well as stained and finished, but before they are assembled with the bolts.

all of this together and adjust for table height from 2 in. to 32 in. as desired.

Attach head bracket to upper ends of legs and clamp. Lay table top across hands; clamp if necessary, loosen leg scissor joint and readjust. You can then drill all the ¼ in. holes, as seen in the exploded view. From the top, drill through the table top, supports and hands. Finally, drill the shoes and leg ends, bolting them together so that the legs support the weight.

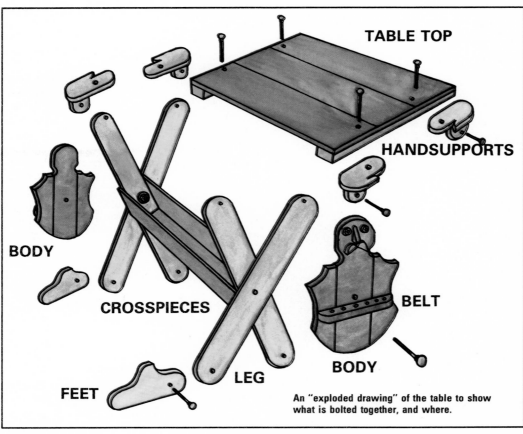

An "exploded drawing" of the table to show what is bolted together, and where.

TABLE TOP

HANDSUPPORTS

BODY

CROSSPIECES

BELT

LEG

BODY

FEET

## MATERIALS
**Plywood** — ¾''
Body top 1 piece 24'' x 66''
**Boards** — ¾'' —
Dry, select pine or fir
1'' x 6'' — 19 linear feet
1'' x 8'' — 6 linear feet
1'' x 2'' — 5 linear feet
**Carriage Bolts:** 6¼'' x 3¼''; 8¼'' x 2''
**Miscellaneous:**
Glue, stain, sealer, varnish or urethane coating, color paint, upholstery tack, 4 checkers, sandpaper.

# Clever max for children

Even the smallest children's room has enough space for "Max." The desk is held horizontal by a cord for homework or play, but it can also be folded down for use as a blackboard.

The basic figure, arms, and the desk top, are outlined on a sheet of ⅜ in. plywood (see drawing on Page 83) and sawn out with a jigsaw. Sand the edges well to eliminate splinters.

The shelf unit can be made from the ⅜ in. plywood scraps. Dados are cut ⅛ in. deep, as shown in the drawing. The boards should fit tight in the dado.

Clamp the top shelf and the one underneath it together and drill two rows of ½ in. holes through the top board, but only slightly into the bottom one, resulting in small indentations. This keeps the pens and pencils which are stored there from sliding around. Ease the edges on the shelves and glue together.

The plexiglass has half-circles of 2¾ in. diameter cut out as finger holes. Sand edges and screw to the front of shelves.

The vertical support in the rear of the figure is glued to the back and secured with a few screws from the front.

The 3½ in. long nose can be glued in place. The hair, the desk top (not the area where arms are to be glued) and the lower half of the man (except shoes) can now be painted with blackboard paint. The remainder of the figure may be stained or painted according to individual taste.

Screw the shelf unit to the "chest" from the rear. Glue the arms to the desk top and insert hooks for the strings. The hinges are best attached to the figure with ¼ in. nuts and bolts, as wood screws may work out. But use screws from the hinges to the desktop.

The cord that holds the desk horizontal should be measured accurately and the loops lashed with nylon string. Or, use nylon cord fused to itself with a match. Staple the cord to the vertical stabilizing piece with two staples.

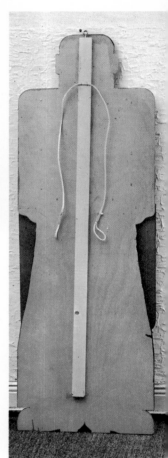

The desk top is painted with two coats of blackboard paint. With arms down, it becomes a chalkboard.

1 x 2 reinforcement is attached to the figure. The cord support is attached to it.

The plastic shelf fronts show at a glance what is available. And nothing can fall out.

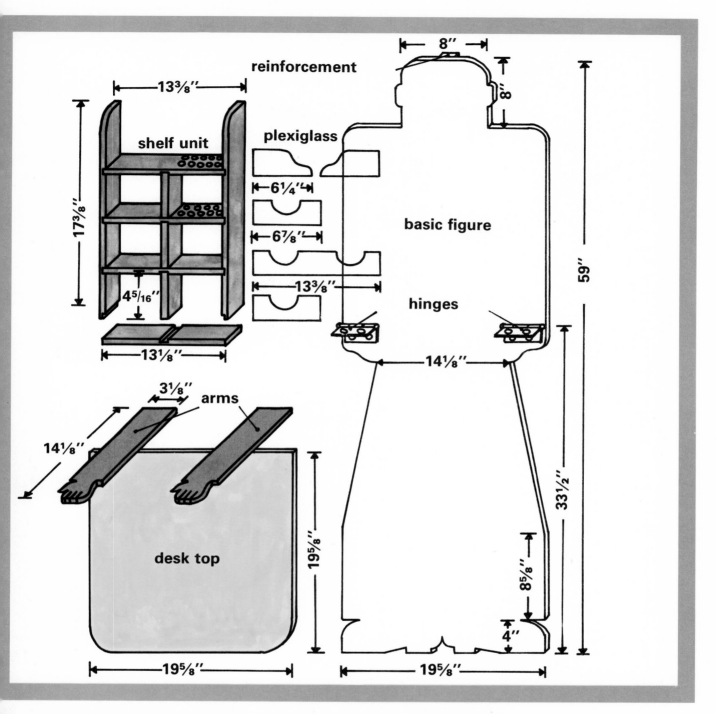

reinforcement

8"

8"

13⅜"

shelf unit

plexiglass

basic figure

17⅜"

6¼"

59"

6⅞"

hinges

13⅜"

4⁵⁄₁₆"

13⅛"

14⅛"

3⅛"

arms

14⅛"

33½"

desk top

19⅝"

8⅝"

4"

19⅝"

19⅝"

The plywood is cut according to this drawing. Everything except the reinforcement is made of ⅜" plywood.

## MATERIALS

1  4' x 5' sheet of ⅜" plywood should be enough for the figure, desk, arms, and shelf unit
1  1" x 2" x 55" for the vertical reinforcement
1  Sheet of plastic ⅛" x 2¾" x 32"
2  Hinges, 3½", 2 hooks, 1 screw eye, and molly or wing nut for attaching to wall
1  Piece of cord
Paint: Colors are your choice

**1** An attractive top-covering and two sturdy leather straps plus a screwed on luggage catch will make your guest-bed look like a "sailors trunk".

**2** This "sailors trunk" contains everything you need for an unexpected overnight stay. T[.] frame and the 2"-thick mattre[.] rolled up inside.

# From out of the box: an extra bed!

All small apartments and cabins benefit from standby furniture that, when not in use, can be folded up as small as our model. This will solve your problem when unexpected guests drop in.

You will flabbergast your company with this bed, because nobody expects that a bed and mattress could be hidden in a box as small as 18 in. x 20 in. x 37 in.

We use ¾ in. pine boards, which can be ordered cut to size at the lumberyard. Watch that the cutoffs are absolutely square, otherwise you will

**The hinge joints for the hinge mechanism will support plenty of weight when these positions of insert screws are used. The screw component with the strong thread intersection is augered and screwed in. The hinges are fastened with threaded screws.**

run into problems later on when assembling and folding the hinges. Begin by laying out the dovetail joints, which are needed for the two corner pieces of the frame. After dadoing them out, glue the two parts together. Now glue on the two 6¼ in. wide boards, which serve as a rest for the lath-floor. These boards should be glued onto all the frame boards. Having done all this, mark the areas where the hinges will have to be attached.

Picture 4 shows you a little trick: you can make the hinges and all the sideboards at the same time, assuring that they will be perfectly level and of the same height. Anchor screws attach to the front face of the boards. Anchor screws are a must, because regular wood screws would tear out after a little while. Once all the frame parts are connected, insert the bushings in which the casters will be located, and secure with spring washer.

After this, the trunk cover can be attached to the frame with a piano hinge (see picture 9). The trunk cover is so roomy that the rolled-up lath-floor and mattress can be stored inside, along with the reading lamp. All wood parts should be sealed with a clear primer and a dull finish stain. The cover can be painted with high gloss oil paint and decorated as you please.

**3** Only the sheet and the blanket are missing here. The trunk is rolled out, and the lath-floor and mattress put in, Picture 8, illustrates how the folding mechanism works. The cover also can serve as a bookshelf, and there is still room for a reading lamp installed on the inside top.

85

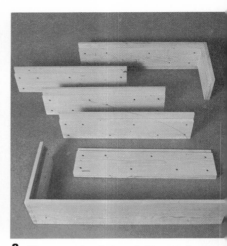

1. Lay out the dovetail joints, which are necessary for the two jointed corner pieces of the frame. After those joints are dadoed, glue pieces together.

2. To give your lath-floor a good support, glue and screw a 6"-wide board on the inside of the bedframe.

3. The corner brackets and sideparts for frame are now finished.

5. Lay out and drill holes for hinges; screw in anchors.

4. A little trick helps ensure that all side sections of the bed will be at the same height: Clamp the two boards together; lay out and chisel groove for hinge (depth should equal hinge thickness). This way you can be sure everything will fit together properly.

6. Using threaded screws, which are screwed into the anchors, eliminates the danger of their breaking away later.

**8.** This picture shows clearly how to fold the bedframe. When folded out, the lath-floor will provide the necessary strength and stability. Folded together, the frame forms the lower part of the trunk. The piano hinge of trunk cover is attached onto headboard of the lower section (see picture 9).

**7.** Use threaded screws for attachment of the casters also.

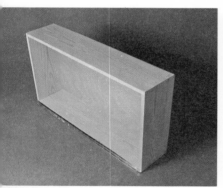

**9.** The cover is of the same size as the folded bedframe. Corner joints are dadoed. A ⅛" plywood panel is glued on frame.

**10.** The lath-floor is made of hardwood laths ⅜" x 1¾". The laths are spaced 2⅛" apart, and stapled onto a ¾" wide strap.

### MATERIALS

All boards ¾" thick: 1 - 9⅞" x 37"; 1 - 7⅞" x 37"; 2 - 6¼" x 35½"; 4 - 7⅞" x 29⅞"; 4 - 6¼" x 29⅞"; 2 - 7⅞" x 15"; 2 - 6¼" x 14³/₁₆".

Cover frame 12 - 7⅞" x 37" 2 - 7⅞" x 19⅝"

1 plywood panel: 1 - ⅛" x 19⅝" x 35½"

18 hardwood laths: ⅜" x 1¾" x 35¼"

Accessories:
12 hinges 1⅜" x 2¾"; 80 screws with anchors ⁵/₁₆"; 6 casters; 2 leather straps with buckles; 1 luggage grip; 1 foam mattress 2" x 35½" x 75"; strap ¾" x 158"

Compare the list of materials with drawings to verify which parts go where. Install a small fluorescent light in trunk cover as your "reading lamp".

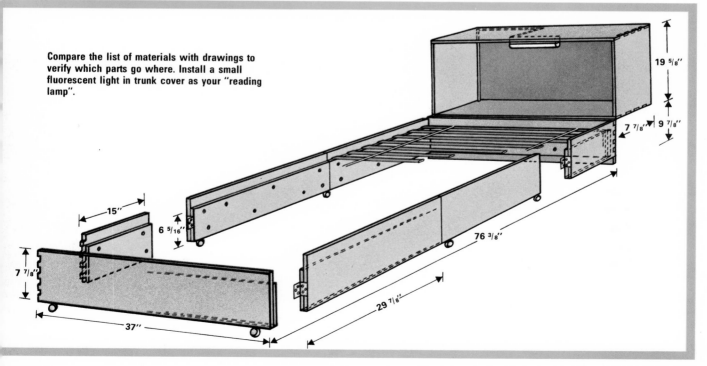

# A handy party table

This table is both unusual and convenient. The sunken center is handy for storage of party accessories such as bottles, ice, decks of cards, and snacks. The bottom of the lowered center can be pulled out for easy cleaning. For the table top we used glued-up hardwood; hardwood plywood with edge strips may be used instead.

The design of this little party table is quite simple: The leg construction is pine and is doweled; the table top and pull-out bottom can be glued together from boards, or you may use parquet squares to save time and energy.

Legs and frame will be flush; space upper and lower frame 1 ¼ in. apart.

Lay out the dowel holes on the legs. To drill

the dowel holes for legs an[d] frames, build yourself a ji[g] using pieces of scra[p] lumber from the legs (se[e] picture 2). Use the sam[e] fixture for drilling all fro[m] ends of frame parts. Drill a[ll] the dowel holes in legs an[d] in the four longer fram[e] sections.

Two notches eac[h] have to be chiseled into th[e] long upper frame stud[s] These notches carry th[e]

1. Using a square, lay out all four legs showing where they will be doweled to the frame. Clamp all legs together.

2. A drill fixture enables you to drill the dowel holes more uniformly because it holds the wood exactly in position. First spot-mark with your drill, take the wood piece out of the drill fixture, and then finish drilling through.

3. Using thin spacers, the drill fixture can also be used for the frame parts being doweled to legs. Clamp the fixture so it can't move. This time you can drill right through without spot-marking.

. Here we see e two drawer ails very clearly. wo laths are crewed underneath e frame. The ottom moves in and ut between the rame. Before you glue e complete leg onstruction, put it gether temporarily be sure everything s in the right place.

5. This picture illustrates how to glue the pull-out bottom: apply glue to groove and key; stick together. To assure a plane surface that isn't warped, clamp both ends with 2" x 4"s and apply pressure. Important: put newspaper between the clamps and the wood to prevent damage.

ross-studs which support he table top. The notches hould be 2 ¼ in. away rom each end, 2 ¼ in. wide nd ¾ in. deep. One of the ower 15 ⅜ in. frame studs vill also need a notch for he pull-out bottom. Before luing legs and frame to- ether, all parts should be anded and the sharp cor- ers on the legs should be moothed.

## MATERIALS

4 legs pine, 1¾'' x 1¾'' x 17¾''
4 pieces pine, ¾'' x 2⅜'' x 29⅛''
4 pieces pine, ¾'' x 2⅜'' x 18⅛''
4 pieces pine, ¾'' x 2⅜'' x 15⅜''
2 cross-pieces pine, ¾'' x 2⅜'' x 23⅝''
1 table top plate (formed from glued boards),
⅞'' x 25¼'' x 39⅜''
Teak molding, ¼'' x 1'' x 190''
Teak molding, ⅜'' x 1⅛'' x 10⅝''
2 teak moldings, ⅜'' x 1'' x 18⅛''

Glue legs to the longer of the pieces and connect to the already-glued inner frame.

Screw two strips un- derneath the 18 ⅛ in.-long lower frame members. These strips support the pullout bottom. Now glue together the pullout bot- tom.

Attach a molding on the front of bottom; this will

**6.** The table top before gluing: use several glued-together boards to form plates for table top and the sliding surface.

**7.** This is the way to attach the moldings. Glue the moldings onto the short sides first.

**8.** The final step is to screw the table top onto the frame. The two cross-boards will first be attached onto the frame and then screwed to the table top.

be used as a pull. The bottom has to be fitted properly or it will be too tight in the frame. Use the same method for gluing the table top as was used for the sliding bottom (see picture 5). Attach a teak molding all around the table top and also on the cut-out center (picture 7). Put the molding on narrow sides first and saw off flush; then glue molding on the long sides. Ease the lower molding corners very well, so they won't splinter. Apply two coats of clear primer to legs and frame, then sand and varnish. Finally, (see picture 8), screw the table top from underneath onto the 23⅝ in.-long cross-members.

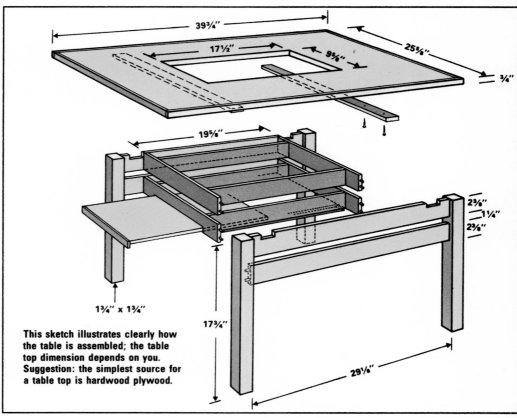

This sketch illustrates clearly how the table is assembled; the table top dimension depends on you. Suggestion: the simplest source for a table top is hardwood plywood.

# A bookshelf as big as you want it to be

Short of room to store books and magazines? Build this shelving unit in just a few hours.

Shelving units make living more convenient. This unit, built of plain wood with nice-looking grain, can be put together very quickly. The material: finished pine, 1 x 2, 1 x 3, or 5/4 x 2, which has to be cut to length (see sketch). Lay out the holes and drill exactly, on a drill press. The hole diameter has to be suited to the diameter of the 10½ in. long threaded rod, which holds the unit together. Secure with a nut on rear of unit.

All outside corners should be eased (rounded slightly) with a rough wood file, and then smoothed out with sandpaper.

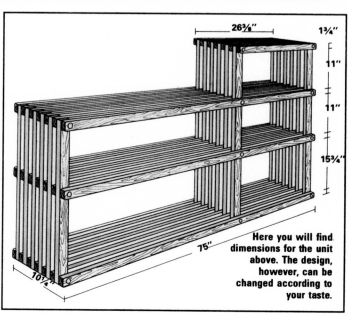

26⅜"
1¾"
11"
11"
15¾"
75"
10½"

Here you will find dimensions for the unit above. The design, however, can be changed according to your taste.

# Living room furniture; build it fast but solid

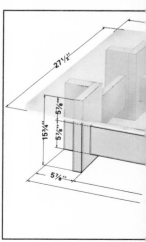

This seating group with two tables is solid beech or other hardwood. The furniture arrangement is unusual because it consists of only two components.

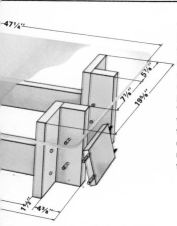

This sketch shows the interesting design of the table, which is also made of hardwood; the wood components are blind doweled. The glass top is placed atop felt strips which are glued onto the vertical posts. The ⅝" thick glass top is heavy enough that it is unnecessary to attach it to the wood frame.

"Basic and solid" best describes the style of living room group. The atmosphere of your living room will be dominated by the dark stained hardwood and the tweedlike material. This project is just right for the do-it-yourselfer: All joints are either doweled or simply fastened together with screws and brackets.

All components of this living room system are made of hardwood boards with finished dimensions of 1½ in. x 5 in. The length and width of an assembled component is 28½ in.; the height of the lower parts, 9⅞ in.; the higher pieces for the arm and backrest are 25⅝ in.

If you have limited access to tools and machinery equipment, you could have all the boards cut to dimension when buying. The boards for the vertical sections have to be beveled on a 45° angle on one side. This way the finished components can be easily screwed together with steel brackets.

For the brackets use ⅛ in. thick sheet metal, 4 in. long and 1½ in. on each side. Each bracket has two $5/16$ in. holes on each side. You may buy similar brackets from your hardware store. To assemble the chairs, couch and tables you should use only ¼ in. screws; this will allow you enough play for a trouble-free assembly. The holes in the wood parts, therefore, have to be ¼ in. in diameter; otherwise, the chairs would be rickety.

**This chair consists of three high elements plus a low one. The seat cushion is placed on straps tied around the inner frame. This frame rests on laths screwed onto the leg frame. The four chair components are assembled with brackets and machine screws on their corners. The bracket holes are a little bigger than the screw diameters.**

94

The shelf unit consists of ladder construction. The supports are doweled to the uprights with two ⅜" dowels each. The four ladders will have a dark stain; the shelves are white for a lively contrast. The shelf boards are cut out at the corners to fit the ladder.

To give the unit a secure foothold, install threaded adjuster legs; these will tighten the shelf between floor and ceiling. Insert a threaded sleeve in the wood. Secure the legs with a nut, making sure it has been tightened.

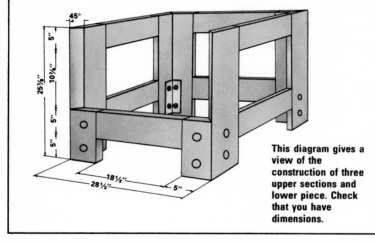

This diagram gives a view of the construction of three upper sections and lower piece. Check that you have dimensions.

etail shows the
rame with straps.
rame has five
Connect them
the inner frame
eather laces
h the finished
f the straps and
them; you will
ome play for your
ns to fit. The
corners are
ted by dowels.

To ensure proper diameters and locations of the many dowel holes, we suggest you build a jig to hold the wood in place during drilling; make it of hardwood or heavy plywood. Start the assembly by sorting out the necessary parts for each component. There are, all together, only three different sizes of boards; 25⅝ in. for the vertical armrest components; 9⅞ in. for the verticals of the lower sections, and 18¾ in. for the cross boards.

For the joints use ⅜ in. diameter wooden dowels, grooved or knurled if possible. Dowel and glue all components together. Excessive glue should be wiped off immediately with a wet cloth, otherwise you will have spots that are hard to get off. Also, the stain will resist in these areas leaving a patchy finish.

Put your components temporarily together and drill the holes for your brackets. Mark your parts for assembly. Moisten all parts with a sponge using warm water. After they are dry, sand with new, sharp sandpaper (180 grit). Dust off sand thoroughly and stain. Try out stain on a scrap piece first. The surface can be further treated with a dull varnish, and later on with a furniture polish or wax. For the final assembly, use machine screws with washers and nuts.

The special advantage of these units is that they can be arranged side by side in many variations; and, if your family grows, you can build more units.

## MATERIALS

**Chair:**

| | |
|---|---|
| 6 pieces hardwood | 1½" x 5" x 25½" mitered |
| 2 pieces hardwood | 1½" x 5" x 9⅞" mitered |
| 7 pieces hardwood | 1½" x 5" x 18⅜" |
| 4 pieces for seat frame | ¾" x 1½" x 25¼" |
| 4 straps for support for seat frame | ⅜" x ⅜" x 25⅜" |
| Screw for assembly | |
| 4 angle iron | |
| 16 machine screws | ¼" x 2" with nuts and washers |
| 56 dowels | ⅜" x 2" |
| Upholstery material with filling | |

**Coffee Table:**
Finished hardwood:

| | |
|---|---|
| 2  1½" x 5" x 23⅝" | 4  1½" x 5" x 15¾" |
| 2  1½" x 5" x 7⅞" | 4 dowels ½" x 2" |
| 4  1½" x 3⅜" x 15¾" | Felt strips for glass top |
| Glass plate ⅝" x 27½" x 41¼" | |
| Wood glue, stain, dull varnish, sandpaper | |

For the skilled homeworker, this room divider should not be difficult. The six elements of similar construction are built separately, then erected and joined to each other. The material: for the sides ½" plywood, and ¾ or 1" multiplex sheets for the shelves.

# The shelves that turn the corner

The shelf-height of about 8 ft. 2 in. can easily be adapted to the height of your room.

The special features of this unit enable it to fill many needs. It can be used as a room divider, built around a corner, or stood in a corner. And when you move, it can be re-grouped to fit your new surroundings. Even the back panels are utilized: two as pin-up walls and two as changeable picture frames.

97

The holes for the screws and threaded rods are drilled simultaneously through all sides. The board on top serves as drill template: everything is marked on it. The boards must be firmly clamped together.

# MATERIALS

Note: The measurements in 16ths and 32nds are the result of metric conversion; you may round off, if you wish, but be careful to similarly round up or down for all like measurements.

¾″, ⅞″ or 1″ Furniture grade plywood, 12 ply.

| | |
|---|---|
| 24 shelves | 9¹³/₁₆″ x 19½″ |
| 24 shelves | 8¼″ x 19½″ |
| 8 corner shelves | 9¹³/₁₆″ x 9¹³/₁₆″ |

½″ Mahogany plywood 5 ply, preferably Honduran or African, not Phillipine.

| | |
|---|---|
| 12 vertical sides | 7⅞″ x 97⅞″ |
| 6 rear panels | 18⅞″ x 56⅛″ |
| * 6 drawer bottoms | 6¹⁵/₁₆″ x 17⅞″ |
| *12 drawer sides | 6¹⁵/₁₆″ x 9¹³/₁₆″ |
| 6 sets drawer fronts & backs (12 total) | 9¹³/₁₆″ x 18⅞″ |
| * 1 drawer bottom | 6⅞″ x 6⅞″ |
| 1 set drawer front & back (2 total) | 7⅞″ x 9¹³/₁₆″ |
| * 2 drawer sides | 6⅞″ x 9¹³/₁₆″ |

Hardware: Aluminum angles—12  1/16″ x 1³/₁₆″ x ⅝″ x 4¾″  12  1/16″ x ³¹/₃₂″ x ⅝″ x 7⅞″

Note: Use the closest dimension you can find. Length is important; other dimensions can be approximate.

Spacer sleeves of 1″ nickel or chrome; Closet pole, 15 each 3⅛″; Threaded rods, 12 each 4¾″ and 3 each 5½″; 27 cap nuts for the above, chrome or nickel plated; 100 leveling studs, chrome or nickel; Round head wood screws, ½″ chrome or nickel, about 70; Oval head wood screws, about 1¾″, chrome or nickel—one box.

The storage drawers are glued without the use of clamps: 6d finishing nails hold the pieces together until the glue has dried. Check with the fingertips to see if all edges fit flush! Immediately remove excess glue on the inside with a damp cloth.

The grooves for the rear panels and base rails are cut with a router

The black water-soluble stain is applied generously with a paint brush and evenly rubbed in with a fine brass brush to penetrate deeper into the wood. Advantage: the natural wood-tone will not shine through when resanding.

After the glue has dried (about 1 hour) countersink nail-heads to about ¹/₁₆ in. depth and fill holes with plastic wood. First test on a piece of scrap-lumber whether the plastic wood accepts the stain in the same tone as the plywood.

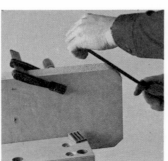

Just as when drilling, all boards for the sides can be rounded off simultaneously at the top corners. Cut corners off with a sash saw and finish at a radius of about 1½ in. with a rasp. Subsequently sand well and ease edges.

The grip-holes (2 in.) on the long side of the file drawers can be neatly cut with a keyhole saw (see TIP at right). Finish by smoothing inner edge with sandpaper and by rounding off carefully towards outside.

*When using the hole saw on a hand-held electric drill, be careful because the drill sometimes is ripped out of your hand when the teeth of the hole saw file into the wood. Also, to prevent splintering when the hole saw comes through the bottom side, place a piece of scrap wood underneath.*

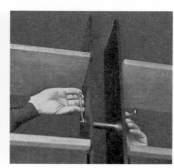

When assembling a unit, first the bottom shelves (to which the base rails have been glued) are attached with screws. The second row of shelves is also screwed in; it supports the rear panel. A piece of plywood serves as spacer between the two shelves.

Each unit is held by ½ in. aluminum angles, which are screwed to the ceiling. First attach the angles, then attach the sides with an extremely short screwdriver. A spacer comes in handy here.

The individual units are interconnected and connected to the wall with ¼ in. threaded rods which are secured with cap nuts on both sides. A 3⅛ in. long nickel plated sleeve (closet rod) on each threaded rod serves as spacer.

This shelf unit owes its smart appearance primarily to the use of five- and twelve-ply veneered plywood. Finishing the edges with filler may not be necessary, but the edges will have to be sanded very neatly in order to display the structure of the layered veneers. The vertical sides, rear panels, and drawers are stained black; the shelves are left natural for high contrast.

The first step consists of drilling through the vertical sides for the threaded rods and the screws. All sides are stacked and held together with clamps. The one on top serves as a drill template, on which everything is accurately marked. The sides should then remain clamped together for rounding the top corners. Cut the corner off with a coping saw, and finish neatly with a rasp or file at a radius of 1½ in. Then sand well and ease the edges.

Prior to staining, the wood must be dampened and sanded to raise the grain. Sand all surfaces thoroughly using fine grit abrasive paper (grain 180). Otherwise the grain will raise again after staining, and result in a rough surface.

Mix the water-soluble stain according to directions and apply generously with a paint brush. Then rub the stain into the surface with a fine brass brush. When the sides are dry, they can be primed and finished. A one-component polyurethane varnish is particularly suitable for this purpose, as it is easy to work with and provides a durable surface.

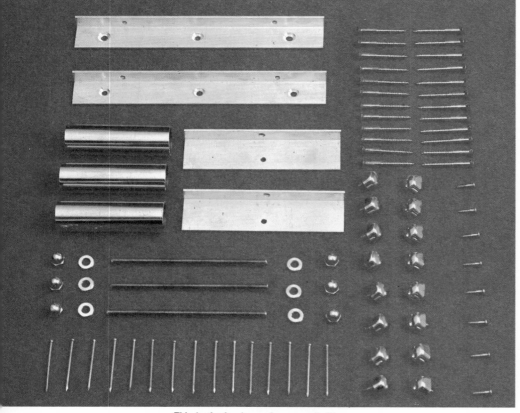

This is the hardware for one unit. The long aluminum angles support the shelves of the corner unit. They are attached simultaneously with the shelves of the adjoining units, so that they will be properly aligned. The corner shelves are held from below with a few screws.

Our shelf is an ideal room divider, as it can be utilized from both sides. Here's a view around the corner to its rear: for the bulletin boards next to the work table, sheets of fiberboard covered with black flannel have been screwed to the rear panels.

Now cut a 3/16 in.-deep groove into the shelves for the rear panels, which are 5/8 in. narrower than the shelves. Do not cut the grooves for the glass-covered rear panels too tight or the glass might break. Finally, sand the shelves smooth and round the edges off. Prime and finish the same as the sides.

The storage drawers can now be built. The drawers are glued and held together by 6d finishing nails. Excess glue on the inner edge should be immediately removed with a damp cloth; any areas with glue will not accept the stain. When the glue has dried, sand and stain the drawers.

Next, the sides are screwed to the shelves. A plywood spacer ensures uniform spacing between the shelves. Then the leveling studs should be hammered in.

The unit toward the wall is installed first. Attach aluminum angle to the ceiling, leaving space for the spacer pipes between the wall and the side of the shelf unit.

Turn threaded rods into the anchors which have been screwed into the walls, and secure on the shelf side with cap nuts.

If later on you should wish to exchange the graphics behind the glass, unscrew the bottom and remove the pane.

The height of the shelf unit is about 5/8 in. less than the room height. In the area of the rear panel the shelves are adjustable with brackets, the other shelves have been attached with screws.

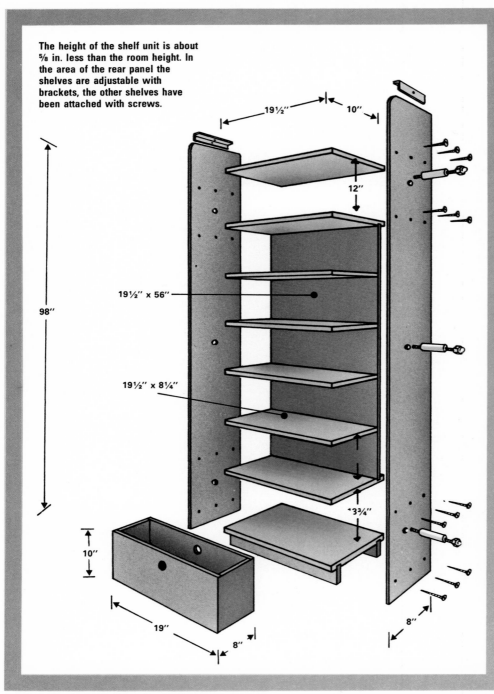

19½"

10"

12"

98"

19½" x 56"

19½" x 8¼"

3¾"

10"

19"

8"

8"

# Swinging Flowers

Bamboo canes, a few yards of chain and copper or brass rods are the materials needed.

This attractive hanging planter is like an ornament for your window—from lofty heights the flowers float.

This hanging planter can be made quickly, is inexpensive, and you can enjoy it for a long time to come because the material is so durable. It does not require further lacquering or other protective coatings. To build it we used approximately ¾-in.-thick bamboo canes which were cut into 12-in. lengths. The rods (or welding wire) that hold the corners together are ⅛ in. or ³/₁₆ in. thick; hard rods of either copper or brass are best since they do not rust. The planter is fastened above window with hooks. Decorative hanging greens that are suitable for planting are green lilies, the entire ivy family, trailing begonias, and fuchsias.

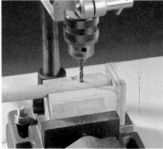

On a notched support with a limit stop the bamboo canes can be drilled without difficulty.

The first hole is pushed over the pin. This automatically gives the correct fitting.

The rods that hold all of it together are riveted underneath with a few taps of the hammer.

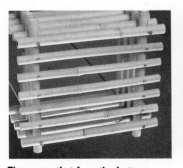

The canes that form the bottom are fastened with a few wood screws.

At the upper end the rod is bent into a loop into which the chain is fitted.

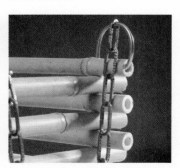

The free end of the rod (or welding wire) is put into a hole which has been drilled into the uppermost cane.

101

The triangular base elements can also be used as seats.

A practical groove joint provides sufficient support for the tabletop.

# Modular Table:
# Little or really big!

The corners of the square abut.

**When a small group turns into a large gathering, an expandable table comes in handy. This versatile piece of furniture becomes an attractive eye-catcher with its unique design.**

**1. The parts of particleboard, which have been cut to the proper size, take ¼ in. wide and ¼ in. deep grooves with the circular saw; apply glue.**

**2. The splines are cut from ¼ in. plywood. They will be ½ in. wide and as long as the grooves require.**

**3. First place one side panel on top of the splines attached to the bottom section. Once spline has been inserted for the other side panel, the second panel can be attached.**

**4. The top piece, also grooved on its underside, comes next. After gluing, press with long clamps (or weights).**

The material for this multi-purpose table is ¾ in. veneered particleboard. After you have cut the components to order according to our materials list, you must complete two more steps prior to assembling the table. The first step: for the bottoms, cut 4 equal-sided right-angle triangles with a 32 in. base, with 30½ in. for each top. The second step: using a circular saw or router, cut the grooves required for joining the individual parts. These grooves, ¼ in. wide and ¼ in. deep, are necessary on the underside of the top piece, the top of the bottom piece (on each of the short sides) and on adjoining side panels. Illustrations 1-3 show how these parts are assembled with glue and splines. We recommend that you cover the visible raw edges with veneer tape prior to gluing.

The tops of the four elements are somewhat smaller than the bottoms because the tabletop, which is provided with a woodstrip on its underside, overlaps all tops and thereby joins all four basic elements into one unit. Illustration 6 shows a "construction trick" that secures the tabletop when only two base elements are used.

Once you have assembled all components, stain the tabletop, inside surfaces, bottoms and tops, and protect with sealer and clear finish.

The scene shown on the sides of the table has been created from a series of photos. When laminating the photos to the outside, it is essential to watch that the edges of the pictures do not warp by drying too soon. Keep the picture edges moist with glue until the glue in the center has dried.

**5.** A strip of solid wood, miter-cut at the ends and into which a ⅜ in. wide and ⅜ in. deep groove has been cut, is glued under the top with the groove protruding.

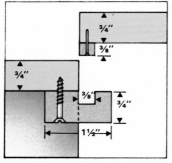

**6.** The tabletop, which has a wood strip, is inserted into this groove. The tabletop rests firmly; the triangular element cannot slide.

This way it is a cocktail table: the triangular elements are pushed together to form a square. The strips underneath the tabletop over lap the tops.

**7.** The wood strip engages the groove of the individual table sections and is attached with glue and finishing nails.

**8.** To make the table portable: attach three casters to each of the four triangular elements.

**9.** The inside and top sections of the four eleme can be stained after veneer tape has been glue to all cut edges.

```
          MATERIALS
¾'' veneered particleboard
  1 ea. 31⅜'' x 31⅜''   Table top
  1 ea. 80'' x 15¼''    Tops
  1 ea. 84'' x 16''     Bottoms
  4 ea. 21⅛'' x 13½''   Side panels
  4 ea. 21⅞'' x 13½''   Side panels
Strips of solid pine
  4 ea. ¾'' x 1½''      Grooved strip
  4 ea. ⅜'' x ⅜''       Strip for
                          table top
12 ea. furniture casters about ⅝''
high; splines, ¼'' x ½'' plywood:
about 40'
```

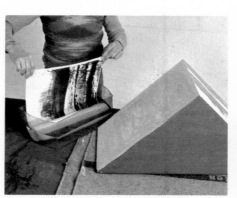

**10.** Large photos are attached to the outside panels: apply glue to the wood, then smooth photos on.

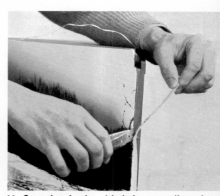

**11.** Once the glue has dried, the protruding edges the photos can be cut off neatly with a sharp knife blade.

Closed, the cabinet looks like a colorful circus. One certainly does not expect to find behind this . . .

. . . a table, two benches, shelves and drawers. The children have everything at hand that they need for work or play.

# Combination Cabinet and Table for Children

This circus cabinet with folding table and benches is just right to cheer up an otherwise bland children's room. Space saving features make it useful as well as decorative.

Although this unique cabinet is particularly helpful in small rooms, you might also want to put it in the family or recreation room. It features a table and two benches which can be folded down. The table is 39⅞ in. long and 27¾ in. wide. That is room enough to spread out fun work or school work. The benches are the same length, but only 13¾ in. wide.

The material shown is ¾-in. lumber core, but regular ¾-in. plywood may be more readily available and lower in cost. Whichever you use, the cabinet will be strong and durable. Not so big and heavy that it can't be moved when you move, nevertheless it is designed for quick disassembly. You can use the offset joiners shown, or any other fastening.

The outside panels of the cabinet are in one piece, and the top and bottom are set between them. Before putting them together rout a rabbet for the rear panel. The routing is ⅜ in. wide by ¼ in. deep. The sides extend 3⅝ in. above the top. The center partitions are also attached between the top and bottom with the cabinet joiners—although you may do it differently, if

you wish. All front edges of these elements must be flush.

Now fit in the shelves. Between the shelves, from top to bottom, you should have 11 1/16 in., 8 5/8 in., 18 7/8 in. and 9 3/8 in. The shelves under the drawers and the shelf behind the table are attached with the joiners or other device similar to those shown. The others rest on shelf brackets. All doors are attached with piano hinges. They are recessed 3/4 in. The three flaps are pivoted with mortised plugs as shown. In order for everything to work well, the plugs must be spaced 1 3/16 in. from the bottom edge, and 1 in. from the front edge of the sides. The height is 3/8 in. lower than heights of the table and bench; this is important. Attach magnetic catches to all flaps and doors.

The figures are sculpted and their top parts are hinged, since they serve as supports for table and benches. With the aid of the grid we have shown on page 108, you can easily transfer the contours to the plywood.

Saw the contours out with a coping saw. Sand and chamfer the edges slightly. Once the figures have been primed, finish as desired. Glue the lower parts on, and attach the top parts with hinges to the table and benches.

Cut the roof of the tent, attach the facing and screws to the top (see pictures 8 and 9).

The drawers run on intermediate shelves. (You can see only those on the top and bottom in the photo.) The sides are doweled between front and back panels and the bottom set into grooves. On all drawers, the fronts are higher than the sides. The handle holes are cut with a hole saw or an expansion bit. Best diameter is 1 3/16 in.

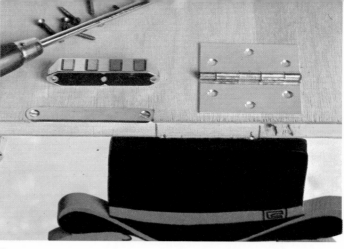

**1.** Prior to cutting the figure apart, its correct position must be marked on the doors. Also, notice the 1/2" space at the fold point.

**2.** The supports for the table and benches are hinged with simple hinges. Heavy magnetic catches hold the benches vertical.

**3.** The figures also serve as handles for folding the panels down. The catch is easy to disengage.

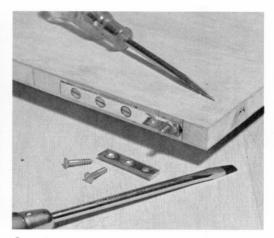

**4.** Offset pivot hinges are used for the flaps. They are mortised. Drill holes for the plugs.

## MATERIALS

**3/4" Plywood**
| | | |
|---|---|---|
| 2 | Side panels | 15 13/16"x71 1/2" |
| 2 | Partitions | 15 9/16"x66 3/8" |
| 2 | Shelves, top and bottom | 15 13/16"x56 3/4" |
| 2 | Shelves, center | 14 1/16"x27 3/4" |
| 1 | Shelf, behind table | 13 1/4"x27 3/4" |
| 2 | Shelves, behind benches | 13 1/4"x13 3/4" |
| 6 | Shelves | 14 1/16"x13 3/4" |
| 2 | Doors, top | 13 11/16"x11 13/16" |
| 2 | Doors, bottom | 13 11/16"x14 3/16" |
| 2 | Doors, center | 13 13/16"x26" |
| 2 | Benches | 13 11/16"x39 7/8" |
| 1 | Table | 27 11/16"x39 7/8" |
| 2 | Figures, R&L | 13"x66 3/8" |
| 1 | Figure, Center | 27 11/16"x66 3/8" |
| 1 | Roof | 15 13/16"x59" |
| 1 | Facing | 4"x27 3/4" |
| 2 | Drawer Fronts | 6 7/8"x13 11/16" |
| 8 | Drawer Fronts | 5 7/8"x6 13/16" |

**3/8" Plywood**
| | | |
|---|---|---|
| 4 | Drawer Sides | 6 5/16"x12 7/8" |
| 2 | Drawer Rear Panels | 6 5/16"x13 11/16" |
| 16 | Drawer Sides | 5 1/8"x12 7/8" |
| 8 | Drawer Rear Panels | 5 1/8"x6 13/16" |
| 2 | Drawer Partitions | 13 1/4"x13 3/8" |

**1/4" Plywood**
Drawer Bottoms
| | | |
|---|---|---|
| 2 | | 13 11/16"x13 1/4" |
| 8 | | 6 13/16"x13 1/4" |
| 1 | Rear Panel | 57 1/2"x67 1/8" |

24 Joiners, 44 shelf brackets, 1 1/16" continuous hinges, 6 light and 3 heavy magnetic catches, 6 offset pivot hinges, 6 hinges.

Here you have the cabinet in all its glory. A great deal can be stored in the drawers and on the shelves.

15³/₄''

11¹³/₁₆''

28''

16³/₁₆''

11⁷/₈''

23¹¹/₁₆''

26''

14³/₁₆''

³/₄''

67¹/₈''

13³/₄''   27³/₄''   13³/₄''

³/₄''   ³/₄''   ³/₄''   ³/₄''

58¹/₄''

This drawing with grid (1 square = 3¹⁵/₁₆'' x 3¹⁵/₁₆'') will help you to transfer the figures to the plywood.
The dimensions are important, also.

108

t is important to sand and chamfer edges well. A wood rasp will help. Now he entire cabinet can be inished. Varnish will proect against little fingers. Finally, after the rear panel has been finished, it can be screwed in. Make sure hat everything is square, otherwise the flaps and doors will not fit.

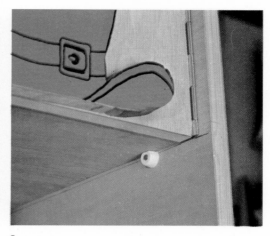

**5.** Top and bottom doors are attached with piano hinges. Light magnetic catches keep them closed.

**6.** The shelves can rest on several types of brackets. They are fitted tightly between the sides.

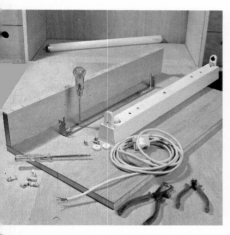

**7.** Indirect lighting is hidden behind a 4''-wide acing. Wiring runs through the back panel.

**8.** Staple a thin plywood batten to the rear of the roof to hide crevices between the scallops.

**9.** The tent roof is attached to the cabinet top with short strips of square material.

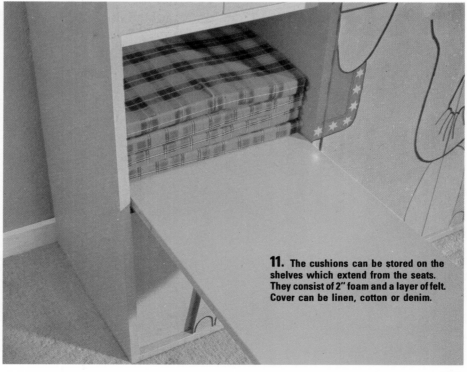

**11.** The cushions can be stored on the shelves which extend from the seats. They consist of 2'' foam and a layer of felt. Cover can be linen, cotton or denim.

**10.** The height of the table is 28¾'', and 17'' for he bench. The height of the seat can be adjusted with cushions of various thicknesses.

# Versatile Wall Unit

This is another project using the Selbermachen dowel system. Here we build a shelf unit without glue, nails or screws. It will help if you study the introductory Selbermachen Dowel System project on pages 11-16.

The project here uses stock that is 2¼ in. x 2¼ in.; if stock of this size is not available locally, you may have to order 4 x 4 lumber and have it milled to size. If you decide to use 2 x 2 stock instead, positions and depths of dowel holes will have to be adjusted.

The wall shelving in the picture at left can be modified as desired. A uniform layout of drill holes and construction of all cabinet units in uniform size enables numerous combinations, as can be seen on the following pages.

Start construction of the wall unit by cutting the square uprights to the room height of your choice. The drill holes are positioned from the bottom up by turning and adjusting the template (see drawing next page). Place drill template flush against the bottom end and drill the first two holes 2 in. deep. Move template up, lock and drill next hole. The locking dowel pin prevents template from sliding; this is essential for even spacing.

The dowels in this shelf unit function simultaneously as connecting members between the uprights and as shelf supports. The four outer uprights are bored with 2 in. deep blind holes; the uprights between them are bored all the way through. The top and bottom dowels extend

A cabinet unit, disassembled into its components. Assembly instructions are in the text.

The top of the unit: the rear dowel keeps the cabinet from tilting forward.

The dowels at front and back support the cabinet unit.

across the entire width.

Assembly of the uprights begins with the individual uprights for the sides, which have previously been sanded and then primed twice. They are assembled like ladders. The ⅝ in. dowels are used here. Now the "ladders" are assembled as a shelving frame. Shelf assembly starts in the center: the dowels are inserted into the center uprights from the side and locked. These dowels are 36 in. long; this will leave 32½ in. between uprights. Now insert and check the next uprights. Each of the four longitudinal dowels is 105⅛ in. long. If dowels of this length are not available, use closet poles.

Shelves and cabinet units are made of ¾ in. plywood. The top and bottom (two pieces each, 30¾ in. x 15¾ in.) are doweled between the side panels (two each, 13¾ in. x 15¾ in.) The rear panel of 31½ in. x 12⅜ in. plywood (or you may substitute ⅛ in. hardboard) is attached in grooves cut with a circular saw. It can also be simply screwed in place. Stain all parts, prime and finish.

Doors are attached prior to assembling the cabinet components; the pivot point will first have to be determined. We have used plastic snaps as the pivot element. The top and bottom have a ⅜ in. hole drilled

Here is another shelf combination; the cabinets can, of course, be placed as desired.

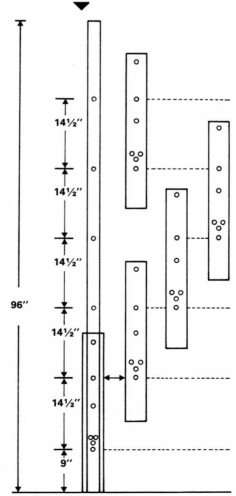

Another interesting setup which can also be used in an office.

The pattern for the drill template; a template assures accurately bored holes in the uprights.

▼

and the socket is tapped into this hole. The opposite piece, with the pivot, is set into top and then bottom edges, spaced ¾ in. from the edge of the door. You may need to change this distance, depending on available materials.

Now the cabinet unit can be assembled. Do not glue parts together; they are held together by the uprights. Press doors into the bottom (insert pivot pin into socket) from the inside. Attach top; slide left side onto dowel; insert rear panel and attach right side. The doors (two each 15¼ in. x 11½ in.) are held by magnetic catches. Use round wooden knobs for handles.

Now insert cabinet unit between uprights and dowels. Cut grooves to a half-round for dowels at front and back edges of the shelves.

The desk top, 32½ in. x 25½ in., is held by two dowels serving as shelf supports. Two locking dowel pins bored into the uprights at the rear secure the desk top against tipping.

The grooved shelf with matching dowel: this serves as a shelf support.

Plastic snaps, consisting of two parts, can be substituted for hinges.

96"

14½"

14½"

14½"

14½"

14½"

9"